Practical AWS Networking

Build and manage complex networks using services such as
Amazon VPC, Elastic Load Balancing, Direct Connect, and
Amazon Route 53

Mitesh Soni

BIRMINGHAM - MUMBAI

Practical AWS Networking

Commissioning Editor: Gebin George
Acquisition Editor: Heramb Bhavsar
Content Development Editor: Sharon Raj
Technical Editor: Prashant Chaudhari
Copy Editor: Safis Editing
Project Coordinator: Virginia Dias
Proofreader: Safis Editing
Indexer: Tejal Daruwale
Graphics: Tania Dutta
Production Coordinator: Nilesh Mohite

First published: January 2018

Production reference: 2120819

Published by Packt Publishing Ltd.
Livery Place
35 Livery Street
Birmingham
B3 2PB, UK.

ISBN 978-1-78839-829-9

www.packtpub.com

To all my friends and well-wishers from my office, college, school, and Gandhinagar.

`mapt.io`

Mapt is an online digital library that gives you full access to over 5,000 books and videos, as well as industry leading tools to help you plan your personal development and advance your career. For more information, please visit our website.

Why subscribe?

- Spend less time learning and more time coding with practical eBooks and Videos from over 4,000 industry professionals

- Improve your learning with Skill Plans built especially for you

- Get a free eBook or video every month

- Mapt is fully searchable

- Copy and paste, print, and bookmark content

PacktPub.com

Did you know that Packt offers eBook versions of every book published, with PDF and ePub files available? You can upgrade to the eBook version at `www.PacktPub.com` and as a print book customer, you are entitled to a discount on the eBook copy. Get in touch with us at `service@packtpub.com` for more details.

At `www.PacktPub.com`, you can also read a collection of free technical articles, sign up for a range of free newsletters, and receive exclusive discounts and offers on Packt books and eBooks.

Contributors

About the author

Mitesh Soni is a DevOps enthusiast. He has worked on projects for DevOps enablement using Microsoft Azure and Visual Studio Team Services. He also has experience of working with other DevOps-enabling tools, such as Jenkins, Chef, IBM UrbanCode Deploy, and Atlassian Bamboo.

He is a CSM, SCJP, SCWCD, VCP, IBM Bluemix, and IBM Urbancode certified professional.

I would like to dedicate this book to my nephew, Shreyansh, who shows me the power of innocence and a smile; Vinay Kher, for being an inspiration for a lifetime; my parents, who silently pray for me; Priyanka, Malav, Meena masi, Jigisha, Nitesh, and Dada and Dadi, for always being there; and the Indian Army and all the brave soldiers in uniform for protecting us.

About the reviewers

Adrin Mukherjee is currently working as a solutions architect with a leading Indian IT firm. He has 13 years of experience and has played several challenging roles as a technical architect, building distributed applications and high-performance systems.
He loves to spend his personal time with his wife, son, and best friend, Choco, a Labrador Retriever.

Zoltan Altfatter (@altfatterz) is a software engineer and AWS certified solutions architect (associate), and is passionate about cloud infrastructures. He has several years of industry experience helping customers on their cloud-native journey.

Packt is searching for authors like you

If you're interested in becoming an author for Packt, please visit authors.packtpub.com and apply today. We have worked with thousands of developers and tech professionals, just like you, to help them share their insight with the global tech community. You can make a general application, apply for a specific hot topic that we are recruiting an author for, or submit your own idea.

Table of Contents

Preface

Cloud computing has become a staple of technical discussions, and it has evolved a lot in the last 10 years or so. Whether small, medium, or large, all organizations are moving to cloud environments due to pull factors such as pay-as-you-go billing models and the innovative services that cloud services provide. **Amazon Web Services** (**AWS**) is a market leader when it comes to providing such innovative services. AWS is easy to use and has a huge knowledge base. AWS helps us achieve high agility, high availability, high fault tolerance, and high scalability, and it provides many services that can change the dynamics of resource usage in any application.

AWS provides a huge number of services, pertaining to compute, storage, networking, databases, migration, media services, DevOps, the **Internet of Things** (**IoT**), big data, management tools, machine learning, analytics, security, identity and compliance, mobile services, **Augmented Reality** (**AR**) and **Virtual Reality** (**VR**), application integration, customer engagement, game development, desktop and app streaming, and more. This book provides details on the implementation of networking services with AWS in a step-by-step manner. This book gives an overview of basic networking services, **Amazon Virtual Private Cloud** (**VPC**), AWS Elastic Load Balancing, AWS Auto Scaling, Amazon Route 53, Identity and Access Management, and security-related configuration. This book also contains steps to troubleshoot the issues that we came across while working on different services for this book.

Every chapter of this book has simple and easy-to-follow steps with screenshots, to make it easier for you to visualize what's going on. The chapters also highlight some best practices and recommendations that should be considered when working with AWS. It will help beginners understand and learn about AWS networking easily.

Who this book is for

Practical AWS Networking is only for beginners. This book targets developers and system administrators who are involved in AWS management. This book also targets technical leads and cloud engineers who are looking to jump-start their AWS networking careers. By reading this book, such professionals will fully understand the important networking services available in AWS and how to utilize them effectively so that their applications are secure, highly available, and fault tolerant.

What this book covers

Chapter 1, *The Basics of Networking on AWS*, provides an overview of AWS and its networking services to get started. This chapter introduces you to key services and concepts.

Chapter 2, *Amazon VPC*, explains Amazon VPC and all of its components. We will see how to provision a logically isolated section of the AWS cloud, where we can launch AWS resources in a virtual network that we define.

Chapter 3, *Elastic Load Balancing*, teaches you how Elastic Load Balancing automatically distributes incoming application traffic across multiple Amazon EC2 instances in the cloud to achieve higher levels of fault tolerance in applications.

Chapter 4, *Auto Scaling*, focuses on how to configure instances in the VPC for Auto Scaling, considering how to manage your configuration to make your application highly available.

Chapter 5, *Amazon Route 53*, discusses using Amazon Route 53 for domain names, routing traffic to the resources for domains, and monitoring the health of resources.

Chapter 6, *AWS Direct Connect*, outlines AWS Direct Connect, which makes it easy to establish a dedicated network connection from your premises to AWS.

Chapter 7, *Security Best Practices*, explores various ways to secure resources in AWS using the different options that are available, such as by using **AWS Identity and Access Management (IAM)**, security groups, and other methods.

Chapter 8, *Troubleshooting Tips*, looks at the day-to-day issues we encounter when creating and managing AWS resources.

To get the most out of this book

This book assumes that you are familiar with at least the basics of cloud computing. Having an understanding of networking concepts will provide you with the background you'll need to be productive with AWS.

You need to have an AWS account to perform the steps mentioned in this book. AWS provides a free trial for one year; this will suffice.

Additionally, you will need access to the internet to download PuTTY to connect to instances. Any normal hardware configuration is good enough to access the AWS management portal from a browser, such as 4 GB RAM and a 500 GB hard disk.

Download the color images

We also provide a PDF file that has color images of the screenshots/diagrams used in this book. You can download it here: `https://www.packtpub.com/sites/default/files/downloads/PracticalAWSNetworking_ColorImages.pdf`.

Conventions used

There are a number of text conventions used throughout this book.

`CodeInText`: Indicates code words in text, database table names, folder names, filenames, file extensions, pathnames, dummy URLs, user input, and Twitter handles. Here is an example: "Once the download is successful, extract the files using the `tar zxpvf apache-tomcat-8.5.20.tar.gz</kbd>` command."

Bold: Indicates a new term, an important word, or words that you see onscreen. For example, words in menus or dialog boxes appear in the text like this. Here is an example: "Select **System info** from the **Administration** panel."

 Warnings or important notes appear like this.

 Tips and tricks appear like this.

Get in touch

Feedback from our readers is always welcome.

General feedback: Email `feedback@packtpub.com` and mention the book title in the subject of your message. If you have questions about any aspect of this book, please email us at `questions@packtpub.com`.

Errata: Although we have taken every care to ensure the accuracy of our content, mistakes do happen. If you have found a mistake in this book, we would be grateful if you would report this to us. Please visit `www.packtpub.com/submit-errata`, selecting your book, clicking on the Errata Submission Form link, and entering the details.

Piracy: If you come across any illegal copies of our works in any form on the Internet, we would be grateful if you would provide us with the location address or website name. Please contact us at copyright@packtpub.com with a link to the material.

If you are interested in becoming an author: If there is a topic that you have expertise in and you are interested in either writing or contributing to a book, please visit authors.packtpub.com.

Reviews

Please leave a review. Once you have read and used this book, why not leave a review on the site that you purchased it from? Potential readers can then see and use your unbiased opinion to make purchase decisions, we at Packt can understand what you think about our products, and our authors can see your feedback on their book. Thank you!

For more information about Packt, please visit packtpub.com.

The Basics of Networking with AWS

1

In this chapter, we will look at a brief overview of **Amazon Web Services** (**AWS**) and its networking services so that we can get started quickly and have an idea about key services and key concepts.

To understand AWS, it is better to have a core understanding of what exactly it is and then look at AWS-related topics.

Cloud computing, cloud service models, cloud deployment models, and cloud characteristics that are based on the **National Institute of Standards and Technology** (**NIST**) definition will help us understand the core of cloud computing. This chapter will cover how we can categorize different services of AWS by considering cloud service models and cloud deployment models.

In this chapter, we will cover the following topics in detail:

- The core concepts of AWS
- Regions and Availability Zones
- Security and compliance
- **Amazon Elastic Compute Cloud** (**Amazon EC2**)
- Security groups
- An overview of networking services
- **Amazon Virtual Private Cloud** (**Amazon VPC**)
- Amazon CloudFront
- Amazon Route 53
- AWS Direct Connect
- Elastic Load Balancing
- Auto Scaling

- Billing Dashboard
- AWS **Total Cost of Ownership** (**TCO**) calculator
- Architecture—compute and networking services for a sample application

Introducing cloud computing

Cloud computing is an on-demand computing resource that provides multi-tenant or dedicated computing resources, such as compute, storage, and network, which are delivered to users over the network.

A network in the form of internet or LAN is based on the deployment model of the cloud. According to NIST's definition of cloud computing, it has both cloud deployment models and cloud service models:

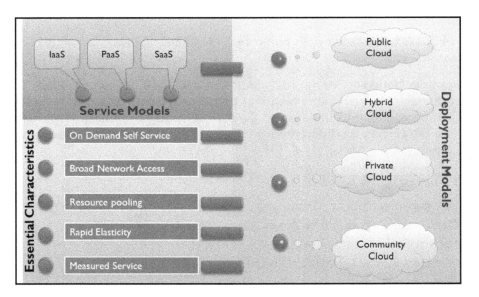

Cloud deployment models define the way resources are deployed, that is, whether they are accessible over LAN or accessible over the internet. There are four cloud deployment models:

- **Public cloud**, which is accessible over the internet
- **Private cloud**, which is accessible over LAN and owned by an organization

- **Community cloud**, where resources are shared by a specific set of organizations that share similar types of interests
- **Hybrid cloud**, which combines two or more deployment models to form a cloud based on specific use cases such as databases that are on-premise due to security reasons

The cloud service model defines the way cloud resources are used by taking into consideration their flexibility or the options that are provided to users. There are three cloud service models:

- **Infrastructure as a Service (IaaS)**: Resources such as compute, storage, and network are accessible to users. Security and control is in the hands of users. The cloud service provider plays a limited role in resource management in this service model.
- **Platform as a Service (PaaS)**: Users get a platform where he/she can deploy a package directly without worrying about setting up a runtime environment. Security and control is in the hands of the cloud service provider. Users can do some configuration for versions of the web server, enable logs, set up load balancers, and so on. Users play a limited role in resource management in this service model.
- **Software as a Service (SaaS)**: The user creates an account, and all of the services are available directly. Office 365, Google Docs, and Zoho Docs are some popular examples of SaaS. The cloud service provider is responsible for resource management in this service model.

Cloud computing has a few characteristics that are significant, such as the multi-tenancy, pay as you go billing model that is similar to electricity billing; an on-demand self service; resource pooling for better utilization of cloud resources; rapid elasticity for scaling up and scaling down instances that are served in case of IaaS or PaaS based on needs in an automated manner; and measured services for billing.

There are many cloud service providers that provide public cloud services in the market. However, among all the providers, **Amazon Web Services** (**AWS**) has established itself as a leader in terms of innovation and the services it provides.

This all began in 2006 when AWS started providing infrastructure services.

Now, AWS services are utilized in more than 190 countries all over the world, and many research firms have announced AWS as a leader in the cloud space as well.

Regions and Availability Zones

The AWS Cloud operates in 16 geographic Regions, with 44 Availability Zones around the world. Some of these are depicted in the following diagram:

 For more details, visit the following website: `https://aws.amazon.com/about-aws/global-infrastructure/`.

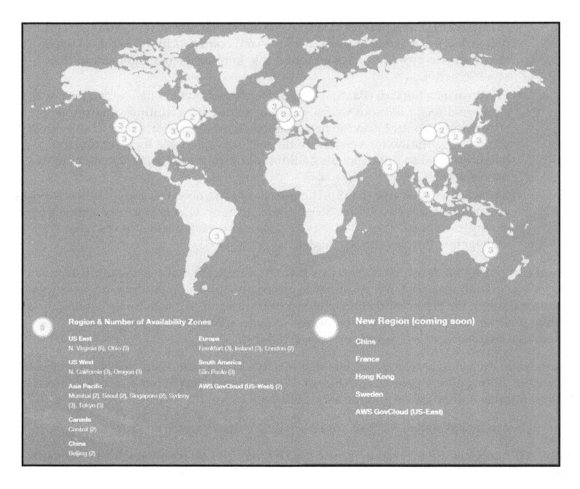

Region & Number of Availability Zones

US East
N. Virginia (6), Ohio (3)

US West
N. California (3), Oregon (3)

Asia Pacific
Mumbai (2), Seoul (2), Singapore (2), Sydney (3), Tokyo (3)

Canada
Central (2)

China
Beijing (2)

Europe
Frankfurt (3), Ireland (3), London (2)

South America
São Paulo (3)

AWS GovCloud (US-West) (2)

New Region (coming soon)

China

France

Hong Kong

Sweden

AWS GovCloud (US-East)

A Region is a location in any part of the world, whereas **Availability Zones (AZs)** are separate data centers that are available in a specific region:

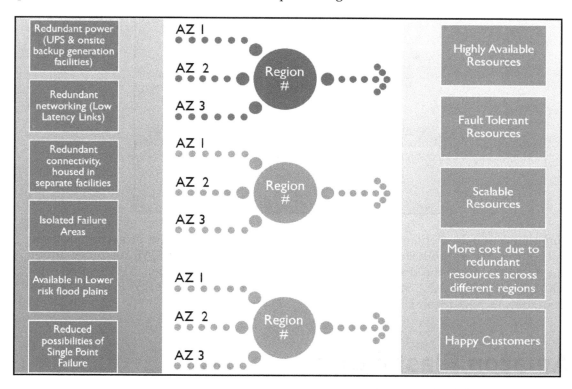

Each region is isolated from another region, and each Availability Zone is planned as an independent failure zone to support highly available resources, fault-tolerant resources, and scalable application architecture.

Security and compliance

Security in AWS is a shared responsibility based on the cloud service model that's used by the customer or user. In AWS, physical resources, such as servers, storage, and the network, are managed by AWS. Users don't have to worry about security since AWS has already put in best practices and it is transparent.

It is up to you to configure security in AWS as per the proven best practices that are available for the AWS infrastructure.

Users can configure security groups and access control lists, **Virtual Private Cloud** (**VPC**), and identity and access management to make the resources in the cloud more secure:

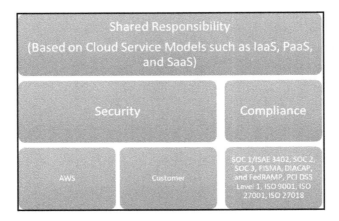

Compliance is extremely important for the assurance of security and protection. Security and compliance are both shared responsibilities for AWS and the AWS customer, and is based on how much the cloud service model is used by the customer. AWS complies to SOC 1/ISAE 3402, SOC 2, SOC 3, FISMA, DIACAP, FedRAMP, PCI DSS Level 1, ISO 9001, ISO 27001, ISO 27018, and so on.

Amazon Elastic Compute Cloud

Amazon **Elastic Compute Cloud** (**EC2**) is a web service. Do you remember Amazon Web Services?

Amazon EC2 provides compute services in the Amazon Cloud.

Is it easy to get your hands on it?

Yes; you can create an account and use the free tier to create a simple instance:

 The AWS free tier allows you to gain free, hands-on experience with the AWS platform and its products and services. Refer to `https://aws.amazon.com/free/` for more information.

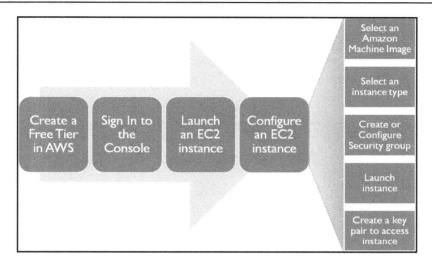

You need to follow these steps to create an instance:

1. Go to `aws.amazon.com` and log in with your credentials.
2. Click on **Services** in the top bar:

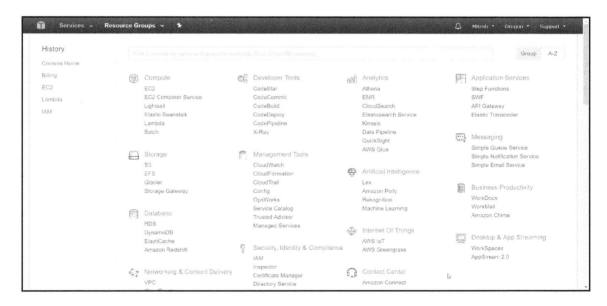

3. Select **EC2** from the **Compute** services that are available in the AWS Portal.
4. The Amazon EC2 dashboard provides details related to a number of running instances, such as **Elastic IPs**, **Volumes**, **Key Pairs**, **Snapshots**, **Load Balancers**, **Security Groups**, **Service Health**, **Supported Platforms**, **Default VPC**-related information, and so on:

5. Click on the **Launch instance** and follow the simple wizard to create an instance.
6. After you have created an instance, the EC2 dashboard will give complete details of your Amazon EC2 instance.
7. Click on **Instances** in the EC2 dashboard to get details on all the instances that you have created in Amazon EC2:

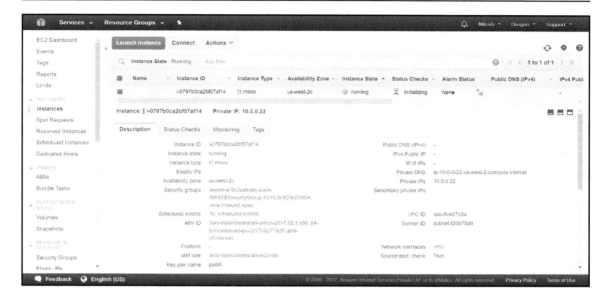

You can edit instance configuration, restart an instance, or terminate an instance from the **Action** menu, which can be found in the EC2 dashboard.

Instances come in different types, and are based on usage and pricing:

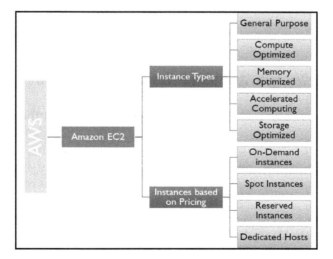

To get more details on the various instance types that are available, visit Amazon EC2 instance types at `https://aws.amazon.com/ec2/instance-types/` and Amazon EC2 pricing at `https://aws.amazon.com/ec2/pricing/`.

Security groups

A security group is a virtual firewall. It manages the traffic flow from and to AWS instances. It is easy to associate a security group with instances in AWS as you can do this while creating an instance. You can assign up to five security groups at the time of launching an instance or after launching the instance. Each security group can serve one or more instances. Security groups are associated with the primary network interface (eth0) of an instance.

Each AWS account comes with a default security group for each VPC and each region. By default, instances are associated with the default security group. The default security group can't be deleted, but it allows all inbound traffic from other instances associated with the default security group and all outbound traffic from the instance.

There are some differences between security groups for EC2-Classic and EC2-VPC. You can find out more at `http://docs.aws.amazon.com/AmazonVPC/latest/UserGuide/VPC_SecurityGroups.html#VPC_Security_Group_Differences`.

Let's try and create a security group and look at what we can do:

1. Go to the EC2 or VPC dashboard via **Network & Security | Security Groups** and click on **Create Security Group**.
2. Provide a **Security group name** and select the VPC that the security group belongs to.
3. You need to configure security rules for inbound and outbound traffic. Based on these rules, traffic is controlled with the use of a security group in AWS. By default, a security group includes an outbound rule that allows all outbound traffic:

4. Click on **Add Rule** and select **Type**, **Protocol**, **Port Range**, **Source**, and **Description**.

5. You can create one or multiple rules based on your requirements:

6. Click on **Create** and verify the security group in the **EC2 Dashboard** or **VPC Dashboard**.

If the instance or the web server is not accessible via PuTTY or a web browser, then you need to troubleshoot the issue. To do this, you need to figure out whether everything is fine with the security group and whether the appropriate rules have been configured or not.

If you change the inbound or outbound traffic rules, then they will be applied to the instances immediately.

An overview of networking services

In this section, we will look at an overview of networking services. We will cover them in more detail in the upcoming chapters:

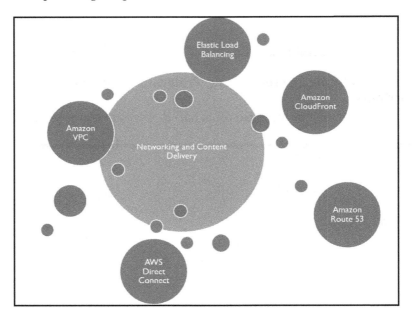

Let's start with Amazon Virtual Private Cloud.

Amazon Virtual Private Cloud

Amazon Virtual Private Cloud (**Amazon VPC**) is more secure because it allows you to create instances in a logically isolated virtual network.

The following screenshot shows a few of the components that are important in the Amazon VPC:

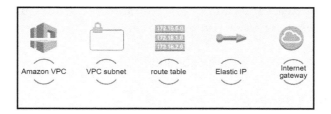

AWS Accounts only support EC2 instances in VPC. Now, do you need to create a VPC the moment you create your account?

The answer is no. A default VPC is available in the Amazon VPC. If you delete the default VPC, then you cannot restore it—you would need to contact AWS Support to do so:

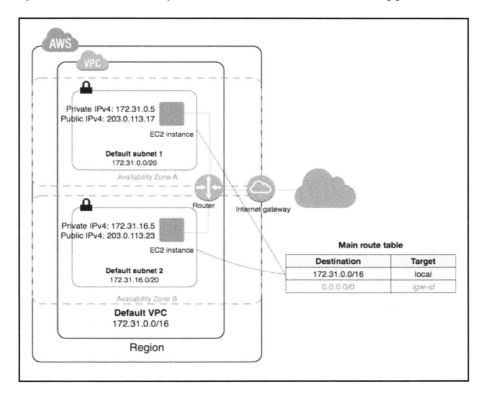

References: http://docs.aws.amazon.com/AmazonVPC/latest/UserGuide/default-vpc.html

The default VPC contains the following:

- A VPC with a size /16 IPv4 CIDR block (172.31.0.0/16). This means that you have 65,536 private IPv4 addresses. For more details on CIDR, check out the following link: https://en.wikipedia.org/wiki/Classless_Inter-Domain_Routing.
- Default subnet /20 in each Availability Zone. Here, you have 4,096 addresses per subnet.
- One internet gateway.
- A main route table for the default VPC.
- A default security group that must be associated with your default VPC.
- A default network **Access Control List** (**ACL**):

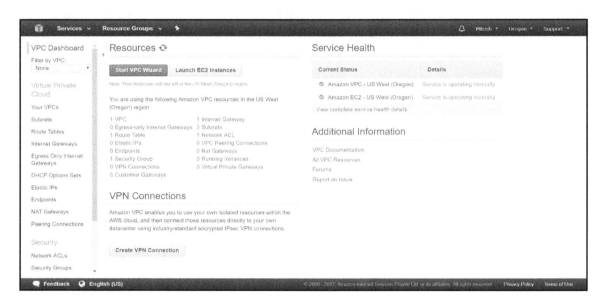

Perform the following steps to display the subnets available in your VPC dashboard:

1. Click on **Your VPCs** in the **VPC Dashboard.**
2. Verify the **VPC ID, State, IPv4 CIDR, Route table, Network ACL,** and so on:

The subnet can be defined as a section of a VPC's IP address range, and is where you can place groups of isolated compute resources.

Each subnet in a default VPC has 4,091 addresses available, and each subnet is created in the different Availability Zones.

3. Click on **Subnet** on the left sidebar in the **VPC Dashboard**. Below Subnets, we have **Route Tables, Internet Gateways, NAT Gateways,** and **Elastic IP addresses**:

   - **Route Tables** help us define subnets that need to be routed to the **Internet Gateway**, the virtual private gateway, or other instances.
   - **Internet Gateway** allows you to connect to the public internet from an Amazon VPC.
   - **NAT Gateway** represents a highly available and managed **Network Address Translation** (**NAT**) service for resources in a private subnet so that they can access the internet. A NAT gateway is created in a public subnet.
   - An **Elastic IP address** is a public static IPv4 address, and is used so that you can access the resource. If an Elastic IP address is not allocated with a running instance, then an hourly charge has to be paid by the user.

In the next section, we will discuss Amazon CloudFront.

Amazon CloudFront

Amazon CloudFront is a **Content Delivery Network (CDN)** service. It helps ensure speedy content delivery to the user, along with the use of edge locations that have been established by AWS.

Go to **AWS Management Console** | **Services** | **Networking & Content Delivery** | **CloudFront**:

The following sequence takes place when the user requests static or dynamic content:

- If the content is available in the edge location near the user, CloudFront delivers the content immediately
- If the content is not available in the edge location near the user, CloudFront requests content from the source, such as an Amazon S3 bucket or an HTTP server, and delivers it to the user

In the next section, we will discuss Amazon Route 53.

Amazon Route 53

Amazon Route 53 is a domain name or DNS service. It is a reliable and scalable service that has DNS servers distributed globally. It scales automatically to manage the spike in DNS queries so that services are robust.

Let's talk about what services it provides to a user. The following services are available when using Amazon Route 53:

- A highly available domain name system
- Domain name registration
- Health checks
- A scalable domain name system

Go to **AWS Management Console** | **Services** | **Networking & Content Delivery** | **Route 53**:

In the next section, we will cover AWS Direct Connect in brief.

AWS Direct Connect

Can we connect to AWS from the internal network of an organization without accessing the internet? The answer is yes!

It's quite simple! Connect the internal network to the AWS Direct Connect location using a standard 1 Gigabit or 10 Gigabit Ethernet fiber-optic cable. Once you have done this, you can create virtual interfaces that connect to AWS services.

Go to **AWS Management Console** I **Services** I **Networking & Content Delivery** I **Direct Connect**:

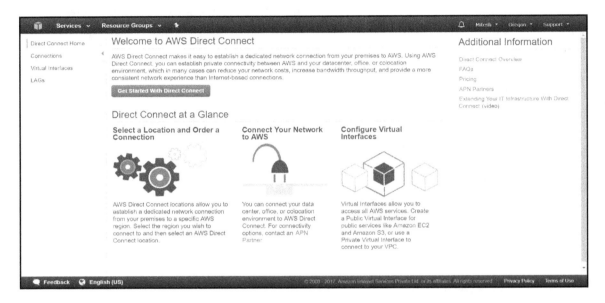

In the next section, we will cover Elastic Load Balancing in brief.

Elastic Load Balancing

Elastic Load Balancing/Elastic Load Balancers (**ELB/ELBs**) can be used to distribute traffic to multiple targets. ELB can be configured on Amazon VPC and Amazon Elastic Beanstalk. It only distributes traffic to healthy targets.

There are two types of load balancers that are supported by Elastic Load Balancing:

- **Application Load Balancers**
- **Classic Load Balancers**:

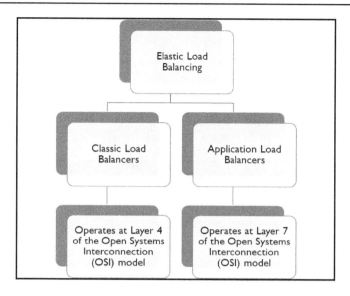

Go to **AWS Management Console** | **Services** | **EC2** | **EC2 Dashboard** | **Load Balancing** | **Load Balancers**:

In the next section, we will cover Auto Scaling in brief.

Auto Scaling

Auto scaling creates a scenario where you have an appropriate number of instances or targets to serve the traffic load based on certain conditions. Based on configured Auto Scaling policies, instances are increased and decreased on demand.

Go to **AWS Management Console** | **Services** | **EC2** | **EC2 Dashboard** | **Auto Scaling** | **Launch Configurations or Auto Scaling Groups**:

In the next section, we will cover the AWS Billing Dashboard.

Billing Dashboard

How can we find how much it costs to use certain AWS resources? In AWS Portal, you can easily find out. AWS Billing and Cost Management provides detailed information on the usage of your resources, as well as budget and notifications. You can also pay your subscription bill from here.

In AWS Portal, click on your username on the top-right bar and select **My Billing Dashboard**.

Billing & Cost Management Dashboard provides **Spend Summary** and **Month-to-Date Spent by service** information as well.

Spend Summary provides a forecast that also takes into account how much the current month will cost you:

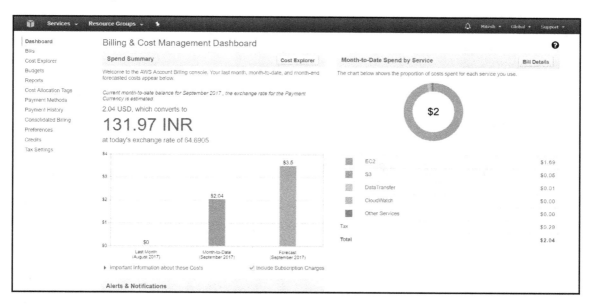

It is very easy to understand what services have costs at first glance.

Click on **Cost Explorer** to get monthly EC2 running hours, costs, and usage:

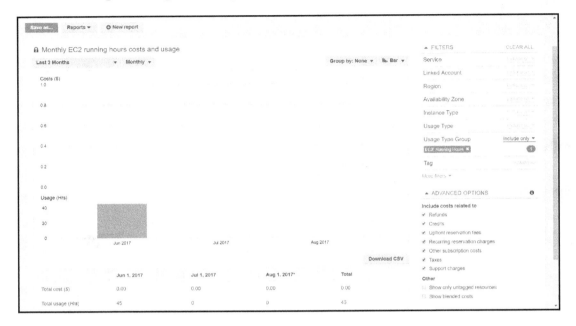

On the **Reports** dropdown menu, select **Daily costs** to get details of costs on a daily basis, as shown in the following screenshot:

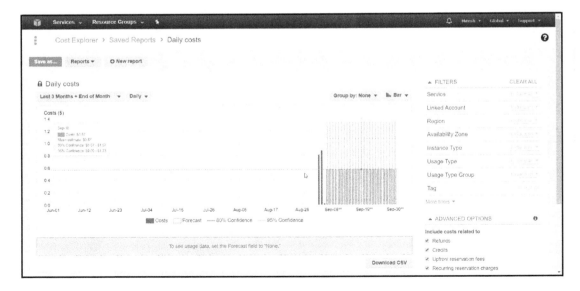

Click on the **Bill Details** in the **Month-to-Date spend by service** section. You can expand all of the services to get more information about the cost that was incurred by using that specific service:

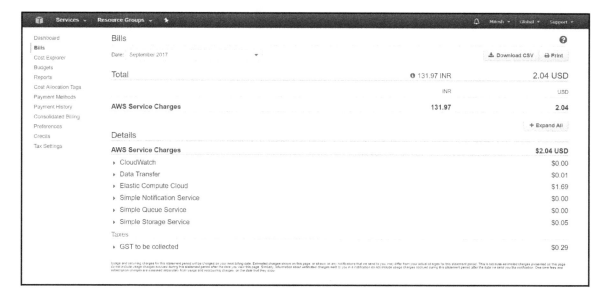

By clicking on the dropdown arrow of each service, you will be able to get the complete details of the service charges, as shown in the following screenshot:

You can also manage budgets from **My Billing Dashboard**. You can create and manage budgets, refine your budget using filters, and add notifications to a budget.

The **Payment Methods** section will allow you to edit and remove **Payment Methods**, and also lets you make payments.

You can also configure **Preferences** to get the following:

- Receive PDF invoices by email
- Receive billing alerts
- Receive billing reports

In the next section, we will look at a sample architecture that uses Amazon VPC.

AWS Total Cost of Ownership (TCO) Calculator

Is there any way to make a cost comparison of the application that you have hosted on-premises and the application that's hosted in your AWS environment?

The answer is yes! Follow these steps to find out how:

1. Go to `https://aws.amazon.com/tco-calculator/` and click on **Launch the TCO Calculator**. Alternatively, you can go to `https://awstcocalculator.com/`:

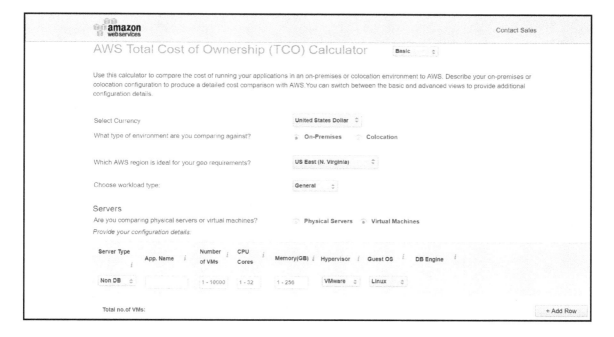

Let's see what the cost comparison is for three web servers with four cores and 8 GB memory and 1 TB storage:

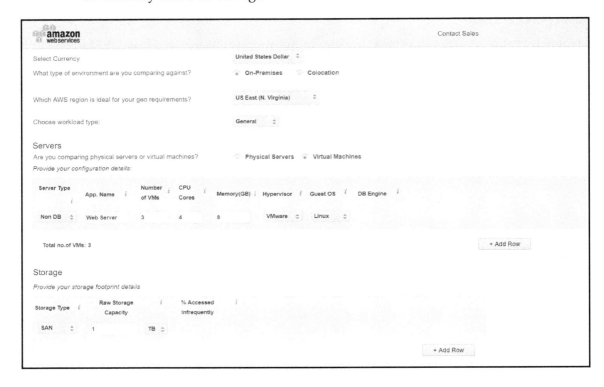

2. Click on **Calculate TCO**.
3. Here, you will be provided with a 3-year cost breakdown:

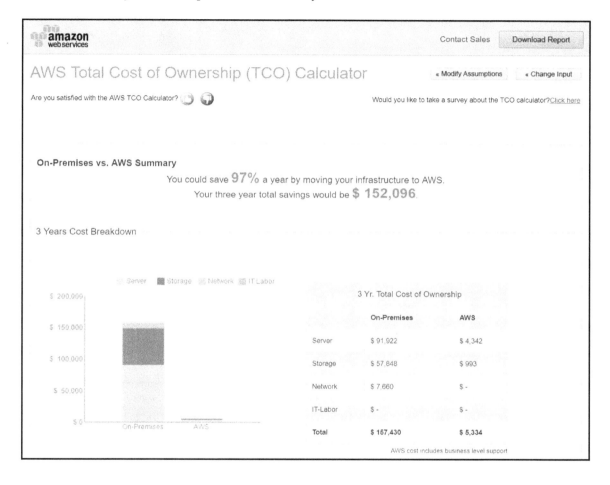

4. Scroll down to **Environment details** to get more details on the comparison of cost calculation:

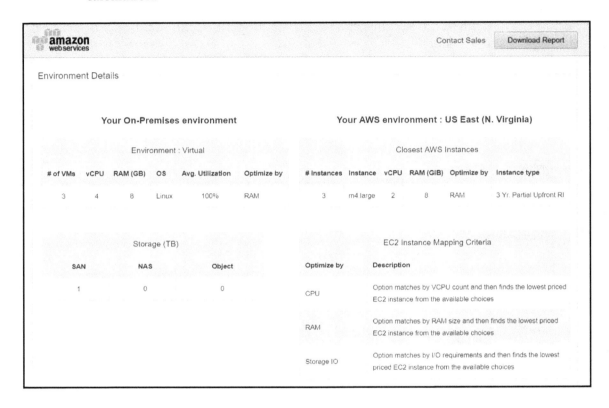

5. In the **Cost Breakdown** section, you will get on-premise and AWS cost breakdowns for servers or instances and storage in charts:

In the next section, we will discuss a sample architecture, including its compute and networking services, in brief.

A sample architecture – compute and networking services

The following diagram is a sample architecture for compute and networking services. It has been provided to give you a clear overview of the architecture:

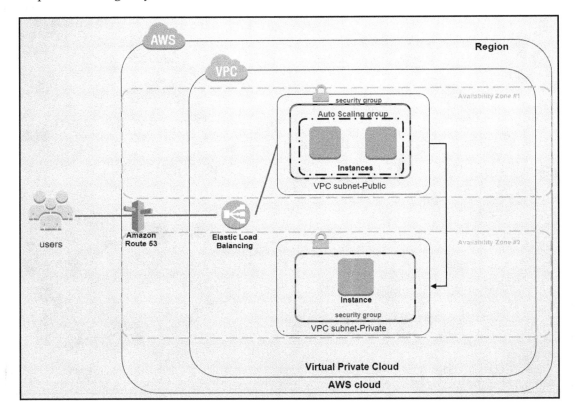

The preceding diagram is the sample architecture for the VPC environment. It has the following features:

- The different Availability Zones for different tiers for high availability and to avoid single point of failure
- Auto Scaling to satisfy varied traffic load
- Different subnets (public and private subnets) for unique routing requirements
- A highly available NAT gateway to provide internet access to a private subnet
- Security groups to control traffic flow

Summary

Well done! We have come to the end of this chapter, so let's summarize what we have covered.

In this chapter, we covered the core concepts of AWS, such as Regions and Availability Zones, Security and Compliance, **Amazon Elastic Compute Cloud** (**Amazon EC2**), and Security groups.

We also covered brief details on networking services, such as Amazon Virtual Private Cloud, Amazon CloudFront, Amazon Route 53, AWS Direct Connect, Elastic Load Balancing, Auto Scaling, Billing Dashboard, the AWS Total Cost of Ownership (TCO) Calculator, and compute and networking services for our sample application.

In the next chapter, we will cover Amazon Virtual Private Cloud in detail.

Amazon VPC 2

In this chapter, we will cover **Amazon Virtual Private Cloud** (**Amazon VPC**) and some of its components.

We can create Amazon VPC in two ways:

- Via the wizard:
    - VPC with a single public subnet
    - VPC with public and private subnets
    - VPC with public and private subnets and hardware VPN access
    - VPC with a private subnet only and hardware VPN access
- Via a custom VPC, without using the wizard

We will cover both types of VPC creation, in brief, to get more familiar with the concepts, and also create some VPCs in an easier manner.

After creating a VPC, we will provision Elastic Beanstalk instances in the custom VPC to host a sample application. Elastic Beanstalk is a **Platform as a Service** (**PaaS**) and creates instances behind the scenes; hence, those instances will be launched in our custom VPC.

We will see how to provision a logically isolated section of the **Amazon Web Services** (**AWS**) cloud, where we can launch AWS resources in a virtual network that we define.

Generally, this chapter will cover the following topics:

- Creating and configuring the VPC
- Creating instances in a VPC

Creating and configuring the VPC

In Chapter 1, *The Basics of Networking on AWS*, we discussed Amazon VPC and its core components in brief. In this section, we will cover how to create a VPC alongside the default VPC. Amazon VPC is secure, because it allows you to create instances in a logically isolated virtual network.

 There is no additional charge for using Amazon VPC.

There are two different ways to create a VPC. We will discuss both in detail. Let's start by creating a VPC using a wizard.

Creating a VPC using a wizard

Creating a VPC using a wizard is the easiest way to create a VPC. Yes, the wizard gives you almost every possibility for creating different types of VPCs:

1. Go to the AWS portal via the following URL: aws.amazon.com. Sign in using your valid credentials.

2. Click on **Services**, go to the **Networking & Content Delivery** section, click on **VPC**, and click on **Start VPC Wizard** under **VPC Dashboard**:

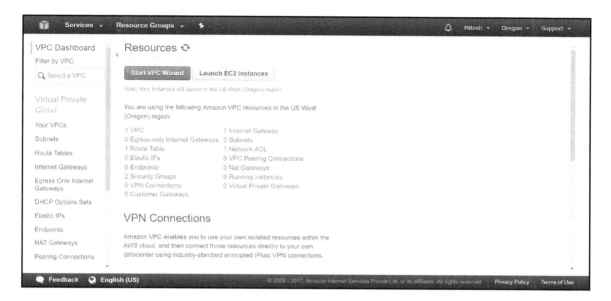

You can create a VPC in four different ways with the wizard:

- VPC with a single public subnet
- VPC with public and private subnets
- VPC with public and private subnets and hardware VPN access
- VPC with a private subnet only and hardware VPN access

Let's see how we can create a VPC with a single public subnet.

Scenario 1 – VPC with a single public subnet

You want to run your instance (IaaS) or Elastic Beanstalk (PaaS) in an isolated environment of the AWS Cloud. However, you want to access those instances using the internet. Perform the following steps:

1. In the **VPC with a Single Public Subnet** section, click on **Select**:

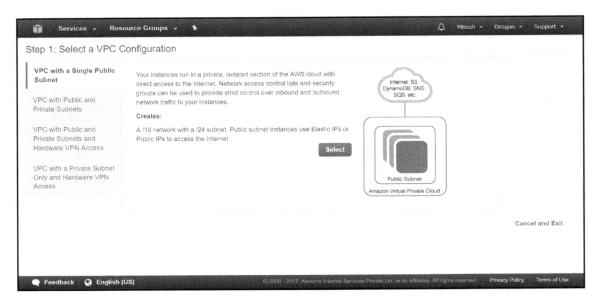

2. By default, this VPC comes with 65531 IP addresses and a public subnet with 251 IP addresses available. You can change the availability zone, subnet name, and hardware tenancy if you want in this configuration. You can also create a service endpoint for AWS DynamoDB and Amazon S3.
3. Click on **Create VPC**.

4. Monitor the progress of VPC creation in the **VPC Dashboard**.

5. Once the VPC has been successfully created, click **OK**.

6. Click on **Your VPCs** in the left sidebar to verify the newly created VPC using the wizard:

7. You can now start creating instances in the subnet that will be accessible through the use of the internet. This leads us to the question of security. In **Security**, you can configure security groups with inbound and outbound rules, and you can also utilize **Network ACLs**.

8. To delete the VPC, just select a VPC and click on the action button. Select **Delete VPC**:

9. You will be asked for confirmation. In our case, there is nothing inside the VPC yet, so we can go ahead and click on **Yes, Delete**.

Hence, a VPC (A /16) with a single public subnet (/24) can be created, and you can create instances that use Elastic IPs or Public IPs to access the internet.

In the next section, we'll look at how to create a VPC with public and private subnets.

Scenario 2 – VPC with public and private subnets

You want to run your instance (IaaS) or Elastic Beanstalk (PaaS) in an isolated environment of AWS Cloud. However, you want to access those instances using the internet. You also want to have an instance that can't be accessed directly from the internet but that can be accessed from the designated public subnet.

In any situation, if instances that have been created in a private subnet require internet access, then they will have to use **Network Address Translation** (**NAT**). Use the following steps to set up the VPC:

1. In the **VPC with Public and Private Subnets** section, click on the **Select** button:

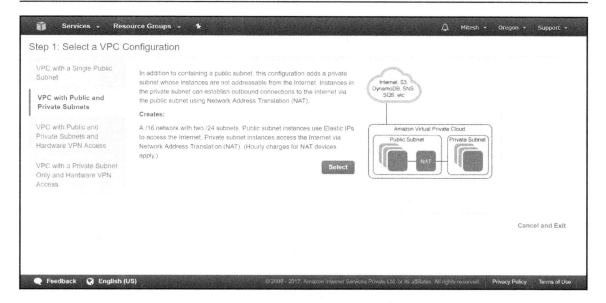

2. Observe the newly added section of the private subnet that, in this case, was missing in scenario 1:

3. Now, scroll down a bit and observe another difference in the wizard; you have to specify details for the NAT gateway as well.

 Remember that the NAT gateway has a cost associated with it.

4. You can change the **Availability Zone**, subnet name, and hardware tenancy if you want in this configuration. You can also create **Service endpoints** for AWS DynamoDB and Amazon S3.

5. Click on **Create VPC**:

A VPC (A /16) with two subnets (/24) can be created, and you can create instances that use Elastic IPs or Public IPs to access the internet in public subnets, while instances in the private subnet can use the internet via **Network Address Translation** (**NAT**).

Utilize NAT instances in a public subnet to enable instances in the private subnet in order to initiate access to the internet or other AWS services. However, it doesn't allow inbound traffic. The major difference is that it is managed by users, while the NAT gateway is managed by AWS and is highly available.

Let's see how to create a VPC with public and private subnets and hardware VPN access.

Scenario 3 – VPC with public and private subnets and hardware VPN access

You want to run your instance (IaaS) or Elastic Beanstalk (PaaS) in an isolated environment of AWS Cloud. However, you want to access those instances using the internet. You also want to have an instance that can't be accessed directly from the internet but that can be accessed from a designated public subnet. Additionally, you want to extend your existing data center to Amazon VPC by creating an IPsec **Virtual Private Network (VPN)** connection between them:

1. In the **VPC with Public and Private Subnets and Hardware VPN Access** section, click on **Select**:

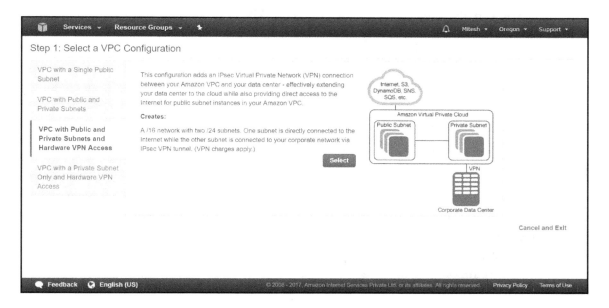

2. Observe the newly added section of the private subnet that, in this case, was missing in scenario 1:

3. You can also create service endpoints for AWS DynamoDB and Amazon S3. You can change the availability zone, subnet name, and hardware tenancy if you want in this configuration.
4. Click on **Next**.
5. Here, you need to provide configuration details for your VPN router or customer gateway.
6. Click on **Create VPC**.

In brief, here is how to configure a site-to-site IPsec VPN to the Amazon AWS VPN gateway:

- Create a virtual private gateway—the remote side of the IPsec VPN connection
- Create the customer gateway—the on-premises side of the IPsec VPN connection
- Create a VPN connection—to connect the customer gateway and the virtual private gateway
- Configure on-premises devices for a site-to-site VPN connection

Hence, a VPC (A /16) with two /24 subnets can be created, and you can create instances that use Elastic IPs or Public IPs to access the internet. The private subnet is connected to the on-premises data center using the IPsec VPN tunnel.

Let's see how we can create a VPC with a private subnet only and hardware VPN access.

Scenario 4 – VPC with a private subnet only and hardware VPN access

Here, you want to have instances that can't be accessed directly. Additionally, you want to extend your existing data center to Amazon VPC by creating an IPsec VPN connection between them:

1. In the **VPC with a Private Subnet Only and Hardware VPN Access** section, click on **Select**:

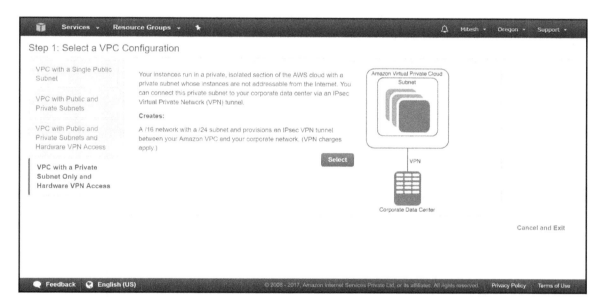

2. You can change the availability zone, subnet name, and hardware tenancy if you want in this configuration. You can also create **Service Endpoints** for AWS DynamoDB and Amazon S3. Only the private subnet section exists in this scenario.
3. Click on **Next**.

4. Here, you need to provide configuration details for your VPN router or customer gateway.
5. Click on **Create VPC**.

A VPC (A /16) with a single subnet can be created. The private subnet is connected to the on-premises data center using the IPsec VPN tunnel.

In the next section, we will create a VPC without using a wizard.

Creating a VPC without using the wizard

Let's create a VPC without using the wizard to understand things in detail and to find out how it works internally. After you have followed the next set of steps, the cloud map will look something like this:

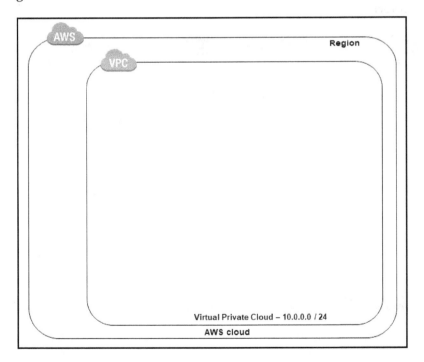

1. Go to the AWS portal by using the URL `aws.amazon.com`. Sign in using your valid credentials.

>   The default limit for the VPCs per region is 5.

2. Click on **Services** | **Networking & Content Delivery** | **VPC**, and then click on **Your VPCs**.
3. You will see a default VPC that is already available for your subscription. To create a new VPC, click on **Create VPC**.
4. Provide a name for the VPC for easy identification.
5. Provide a CIDR block with a /24 subnet mask. Subnet masks from /16 to /28 are allowed in the CIDR field. You can keep the **Tenancy default** or change it to **Dedicated**. A dedicated tenancy will cost more, for obvious reasons:

6. Click on **Yes, Create**.
7. In the **Your VPCs** section, verify the newly created VPC by selecting it:

8. In the **VPC Dashboard**, click on **Subnets** in the left sidebar. At the time of writing, there is no subnet available and associated to the `packt` VPC. Before creating the subnet, let's see what other components are created and associated with the VPC we created recently:

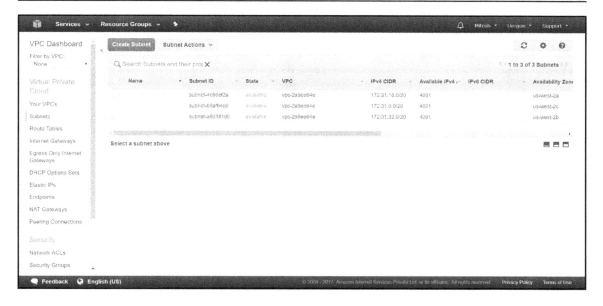

9. In the **VPC Dashboard**, click on **Route Tables** in the left sidebar. You can see that the route table for the `packt` VPC is available:

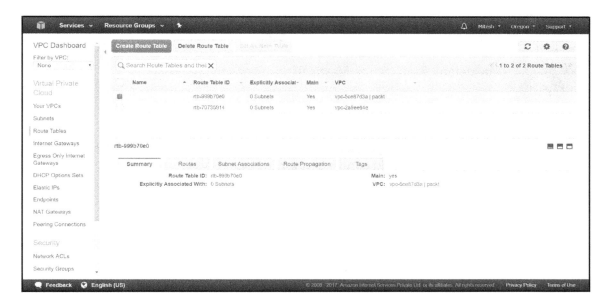

10. In the **VPC Dashboard,** click on **Internet Gateways** in the left sidebar. No internet gateway is associated with the `packt` VPC:

11. In the **VPC Dashboard**, click on **Elastic IPs** in the left sidebar. No Elastic IPs are available as of now. We also haven't created any instances.

 The default limit for the Elastic IP addresses per region is 5.

12. In the **VPC Dashboard**, click on **NAT Gateways** in the left sidebar. No NAT gateway is available and configured for the `packt` VPC.

13. Click on **Network ACLs** in the left sidebar. One network ACL will be created and associated with the VPC:

14. Click on **Security Groups** in the left sidebar. The default security group for the `packt` VPC is available:

Now, we will create a public subnet in the `packt` VPC. The result will appear as follows:

 The default limit for the number of subnets per VPC is 200.

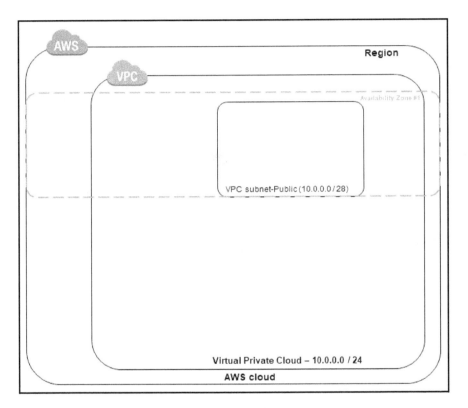

15. In the **VPC Dashboard**, click on **Subnets** in the left sidebar.
16. Click on **Create Subnet**.
17. Provide a **Name tag** and select the `packt` VPC. We need to provide an IPv4 CIDR block based on VPC CIDRs that have been configured for the `packt` VPC.

18. Let's create a subnet with a /28 subnet mask. Click on **Yes, Create**:

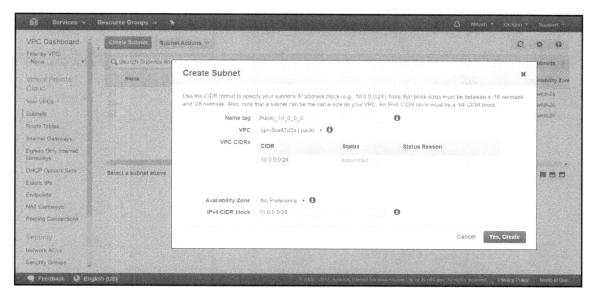

19. What if you want to create a subnet in a specific availability zone? Simple—select the availability zone:

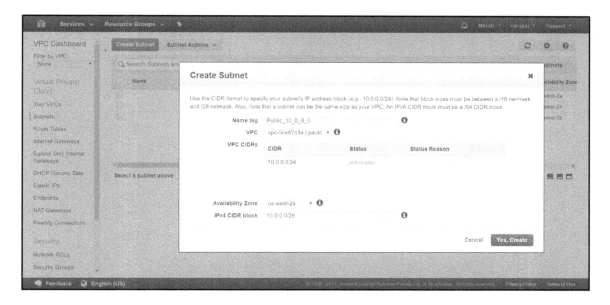

20. Go to the **Subnets** section and verify the newly created subnet that is associated with the `packt` VPC.

21. We would like to utilize this subnet as a public subnet:

Let's create a private subnet that will be utilized as a private subnet. The result will appear as follows:

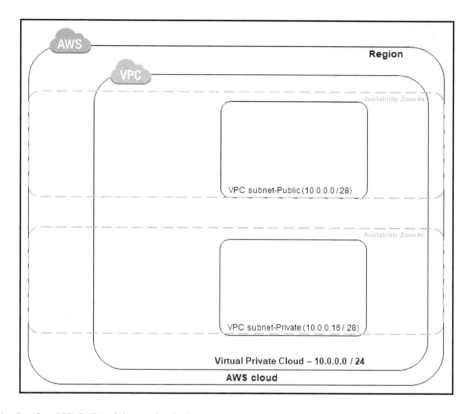

1. In the **VPC Dashboard**, click on subnets in the left sidebar.
2. Click on **Create Subnet**.
3. Provide a **Name tag** and select the `packt` VPC. We need to provide an IPv4 CIDR block based on VPC CIDRs that have been configured for the `packt` VPC.

Let's create a subnet with a /28 subnet mask. We need to provide a CIDR block that doesn't overlap pre-existing CIDR blocks:

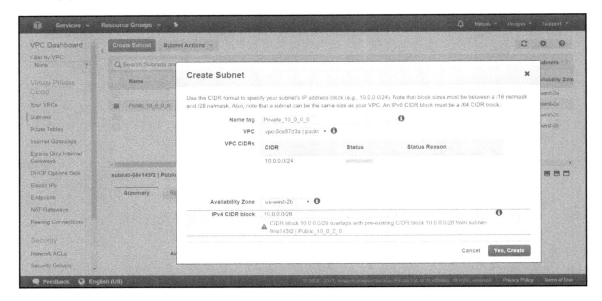

Let's try another one.

Nope. It's not working. Why?

Because /28 provides 16 addresses.

We have utilized 10.0.0.0/28 for the public subnet, and that utilizes 16 addresses from 10.0.0.0/28 to 10.0.0.15/28.

The following is a list of CIDR blocks, with the available IP range, subnet mask, and IP addresses:

CIDR Block	IP Range	Subnet Mask	IP Quantity
10.0.0.0/32	10.0.0.0 - 10.0.0.0	255.255.255.255	1
10.0.0.0/31	10.0.0.0 - 10.0.0.1	255.255.255.254	2
10.0.0.0/30	10.0.0.0 - 10.0.0.3	255.255.255.252	4
10.0.0.0/29	10.0.0.0 - 10.0.0.7	255.255.255.248	8
10.0.0.0/28	10.0.0.0 - 10.0.0.15	255.255.255.240	16
10.0.0.0/27	10.0.0.0 - 10.0.0.31	255.255.255.224	32
10.0.0.0/26	10.0.0.0 - 10.0.0.63	255.255.255.192	64
10.0.0.0/25	10.0.0.0 - 10.0.0.127	255.255.255.128	128
10.0.0.0/24	10.0.0.0 - 10.0.0.255	255.255.255.0	256

Now, let's try `10.0.0.16/28`.

Yes, it worked!

Click on **Yes, Create:**

 The default limit for IPv4 CIDR blocks per VPC is 5.

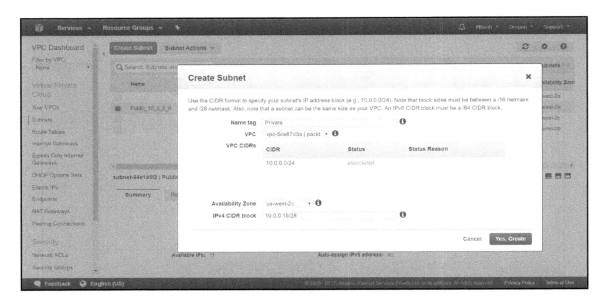

Go to the **Subnets** section and verify the newly created subnet that is associated with the `packt` VPC:

An internet gateway allows access to the internet for instances that are created in the VPC, as shown here:

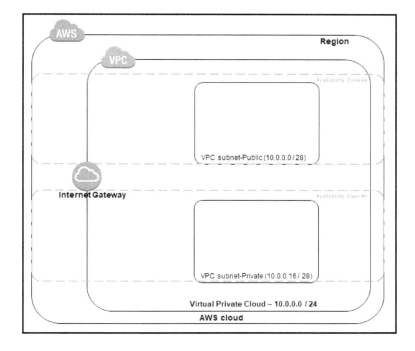

Only one internet gateway can be attached to one VPC.

We will configure the following things in the upcoming section to achieve internet access for our instances in the public subnet:

- How can we know whether a subnet is public or private?
  - If an internet gateway is assigned to a subnet, then it is public

The following screenshot describes the process we will follow:

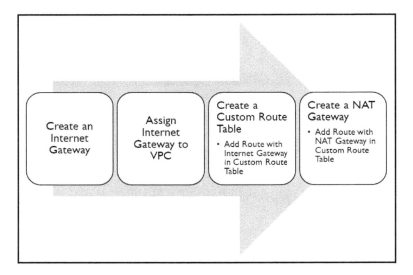

Perform the following steps to complete the process that's displayed in the preceding diagram:

1. In the **VPC Dashboard**, click on **Internet Gateways** in the left sidebar. Click on **Create Internet Gateway**:

2. Name the internet gateway and click on **Yes, Create**:

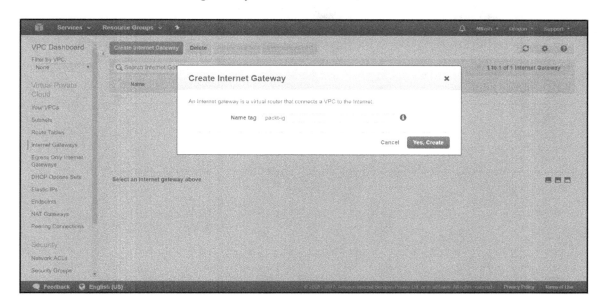

3. Verify the newly created internet gateway in its detached state in the **VPC Dashboard**. Select the internet gateway and click on **Attach to VPC**:

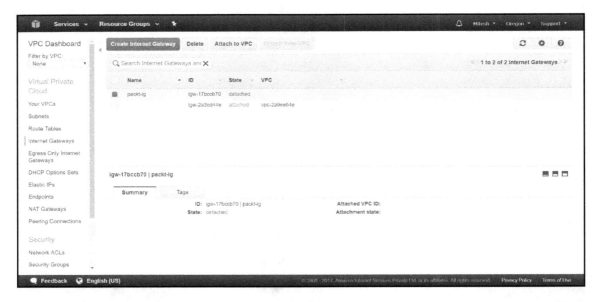

4. Select the appropriate VPC from the dropdown and click on **Yes, Attach**.

 The default limit for **Internet Gateways** per region is 5.

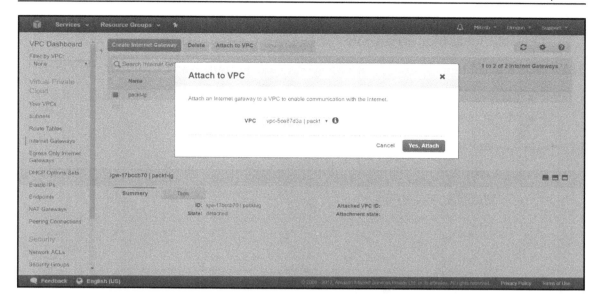

5. Verify the attached internet gateway in the **VPC Dashboard**.
6. Go to **Subnets** and click on the public subnet that we created. Verify the **Route Table** that is associated with this subnet:

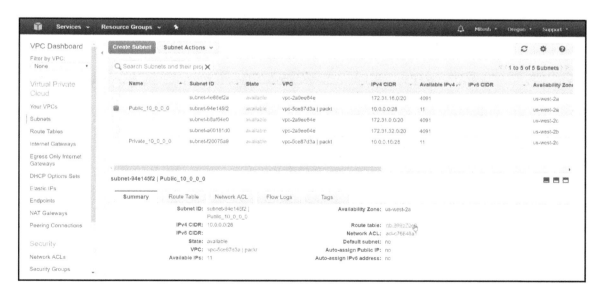

7. Go to **Route Tables** and click on **Routes** to see the rules associated with the route table. It has local access only.

The route table contains a set of rules that specify where traffic can be routed:

- Each subnet can be associated with only one route table
- Multiple subnets can be assigned to a single route table

In private subnets, the route table is the same:

So, the main route table has local access only.

Let's create our own custom route table and attach it to an internet gateway to provide internet access to instances in the VPC. The result will appear as follows:

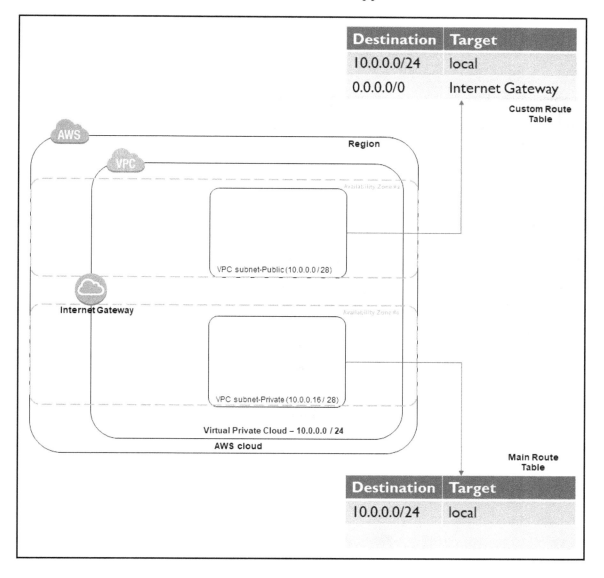

Perform the following steps to create your own custom route table:

1. In the **VPC Dashboard**, click on **Route Tables.** Then, click on **Create Route Table**.
2. Supply a name tag and select the VPC that we created earlier.
3. Click on **Yes, Create**:

4. Verify the newly created route table in the VPC Dashboard.
5. Go to the **Routes** section at the bottom of the page and notice that it has the same access as the default route table.
6. Click on **Edit**.
7. Click on **Add another route**.
8. In **Destination**, enter the value 0.0.0.0/0.

9. In **Target**, select the internet gateway that we have created:

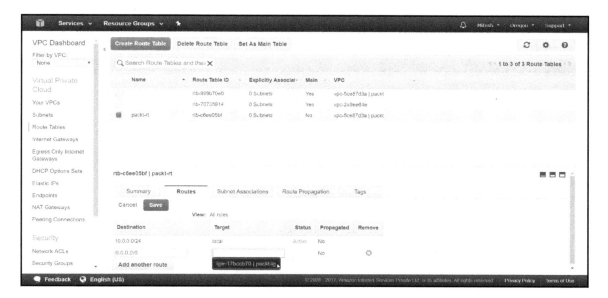

 The default limit for route tables per VPC is 200. The default limit for routes per route table is 50.

10. Click on **Save**.

However, there is no explicit subnet association for this route table yet, which we will create now:

1. Click on **Subnet Associations**:

2. Click on **Edit**.

3. Associate the public subnet with this route table:

4. Click on **Save**.
5. We don't want internet access for the private subnet. Go to the main route table of the VPC.
6. Go to **Subnet Associations**.

7. Associate the private subnet explicitly here:

8. Go to **VPC Dashboard** | **Route Tables** and verify any explicit associations for the main and custom route tables of the `packt` VPC:

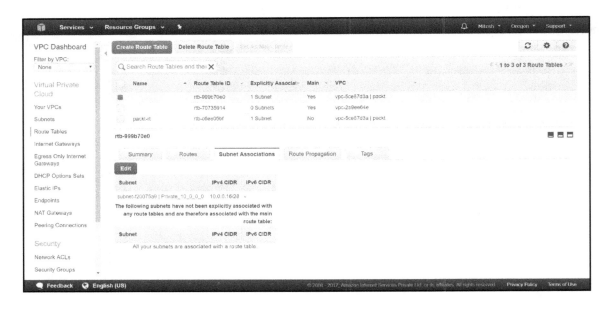

So, we have now configured internet access for the instances that are available in the public subnet using an Internet Gateway.

Now, consider a situation where we need internet access for instances that are launched in the private subnet. The immediate question will be, what about security? We don't want a situation where instances are accessed from the internet. We can avoid this by using NAT devices. There are two ways to achieve this in AWS. One is by creating a NAT instance, and the other is by creating a NAT gateway.

 Add a NAT device to the public subnet. Why? Only then will it be able to access the internet.

We will use a NAT gateway here to demonstrate configuring internet access to instances that are available in the private subnet:

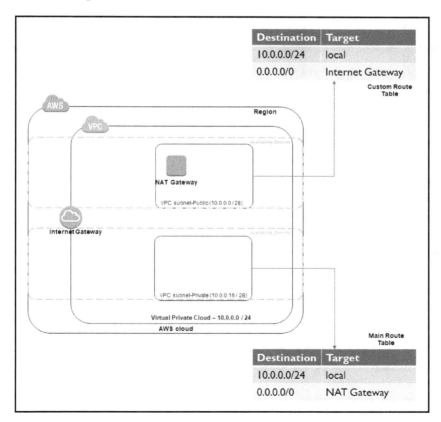

Perform the following steps for configuring internet access to instances that are available in the private subnet using NAT gateways:

1. Go to the **VPC Dashboard,** click on **NAT Gateways,** and click on **Create NAT Gateway**.
2. In the subnet, select the public subnet that we created in the `packt` VPC:

We also need to assign an Elastic IP to the NAT Gateway. If you don't have any Elastic IP addresses, create a new one:

 If an Elastic IP address is created but not utilized, it will cost money.

1. Click on **Create New EIP**.
2. Click on **Create a NAT Gateway**.
3. Click on **View NAT Gateways**:

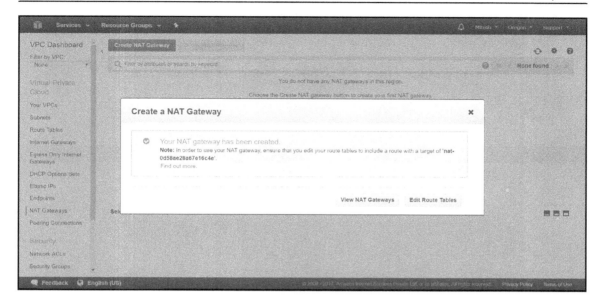

4. It will be in a pending state:

5. After some time, verify that the EIP is allocated and that a **Private IP address** is also available in the range we defined for our public subnet:

The default limit for NAT Gateways per availability zone is 5.

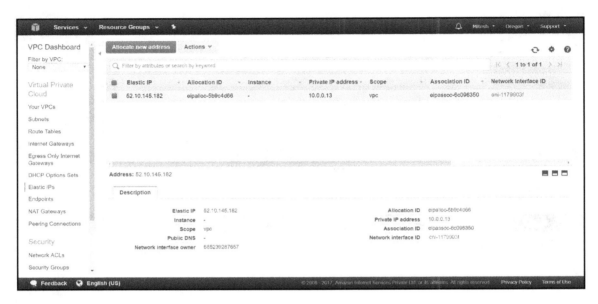

Now, the next step is to define a route from the private subnet to the NAT gateway.

How can we achieve this? Just follow these steps:

1. Go to the main **Route Tables** where we have associated our subnet explicitly.
2. Click on **Routes** | **Edit** | **Add another route**.
3. Give `0.0.0.0/0` as the destination and the recently created NAT gateway as the target:

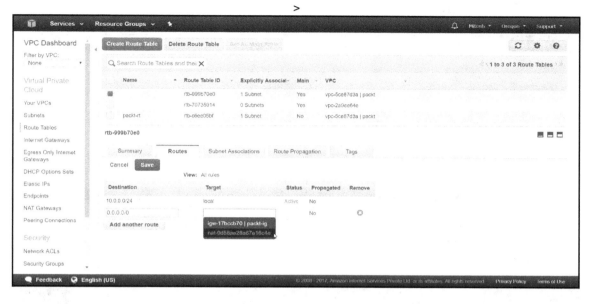

4. Click on **Save**.

Creating instances in a VPC

Let's try to create instances in the VPC that we created earlier in this chapter. We will try to launch the Elastic Beanstalk environment in the `packt` VPC and verify the instances it creates in the background in VPC. Elastic Beanstalk is a PaaS offering from AWS:

1. Go to **Services | Compute | Elastic Beanstalk**.
2. Click on **Create New Application**.
3. Supply an **Application Name** and click on **Create**.

We can create multiple environments for application deployment in Elastic Beanstalk.

4. Click on **Create one now:**

5. Select **Web server environment** since we are going to deploy a Spring-based web application in Elastic Beanstalk.
6. Click on **Select**:

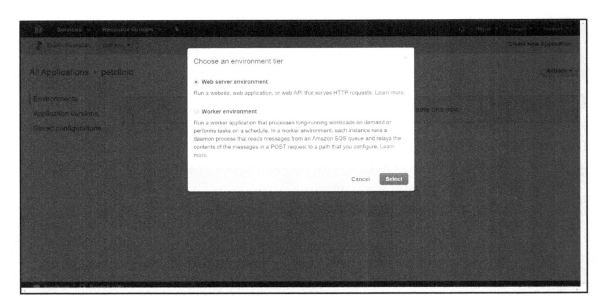

7. Supply the environment name, domain name, and so on:

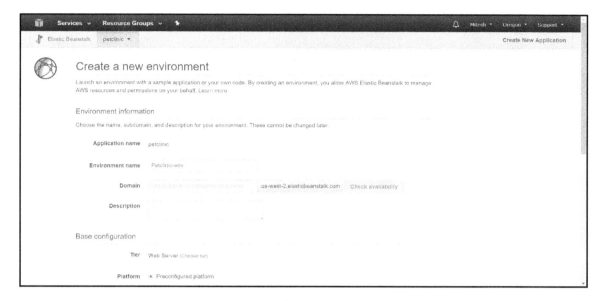

8. In the base configuration sections, select **Tomcat** in the platform field.
9. Click on **Upload your code**.

10. Click on the **Upload** button:

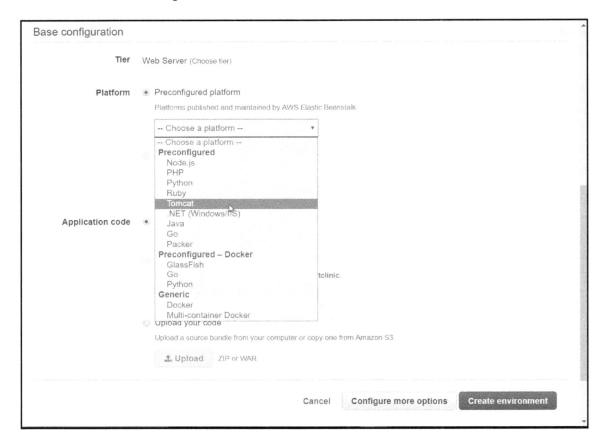

11. Click on **Source code origin**.
12. Provide the path from the local filesystem. Upload any simple WAR file to S3, or choose one from the local system:

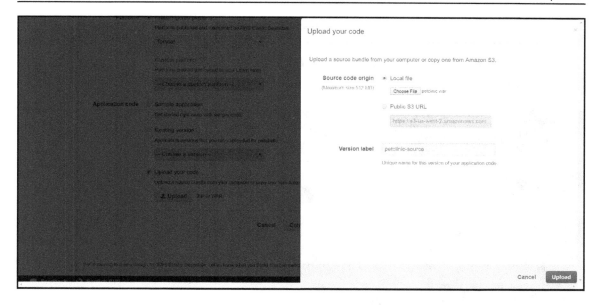

13. Now, click on **Configure more options**.
14. Select **Low cost...** in the configuration preset:

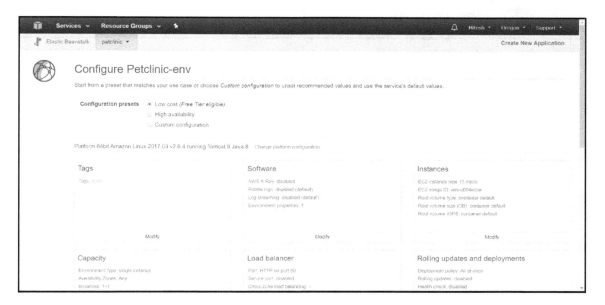

15. Scroll down and go to the **Network** section. There is no VPC configured.
16. Click on **Modify**.
17. Select the VPC and the public subnet.
18. Click on **Save**:

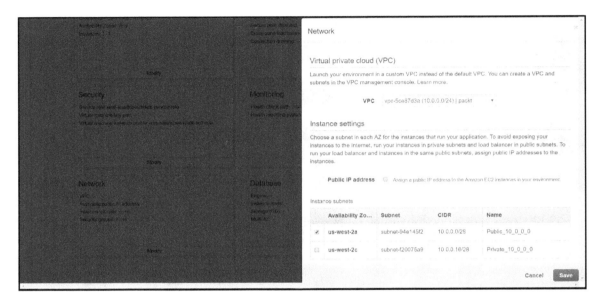

 Each instance that you launch into a custom VPC has a private IPv4 address, but no public IPv4 address. We need to specify it at the time of launch.

19. Click on **Create environment**:

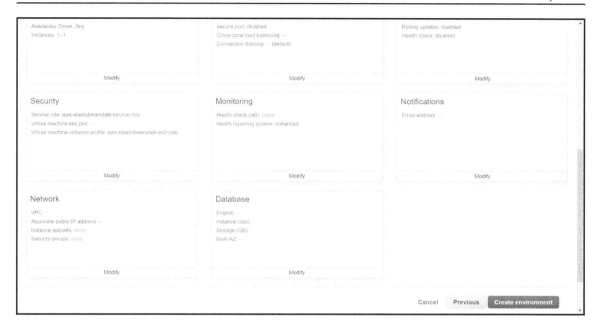

20. Review the environment creation process in the AWS Elastic Beanstalk dashboard:

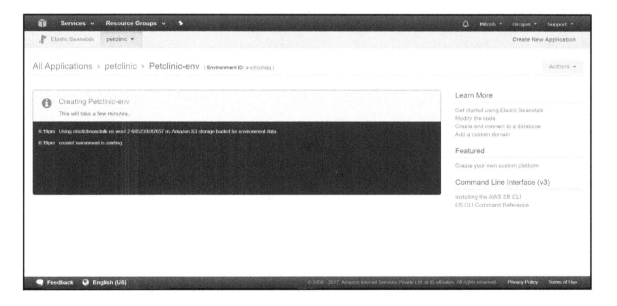

21. The environment is just about ready:

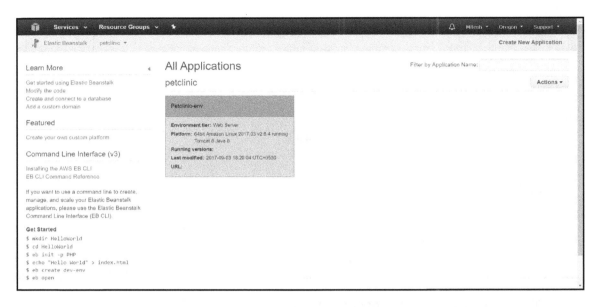

22. We can visit **All Applications | petclinic** to get all the environments that we have created.

23. Click on an environment, and it will show the progress for existing operations:

Let's check the EC2 instances in the AWS portal:

1. Go to EC2 instances. Check the VPC ID, private IP, and other details. The instance that is created for AWS Elastic Beanstalk is created in the `packt` VPC that we have created:

2. Verify whether the instance has been added to the environment that we created in AWS Elastic Beanstalk:

An EIP is also allocated.

3. Go to the EC2 dashboard and select EIP to verify that the newly created EIP that is associated with the instance has been created for AWS Elastic Beanstalk.

The environment will be successfully created.

4. Now, verify the health of the environment in the console log. Go to **Environment** and verify whether the health is OK. Click on the URL that's available near **Environment ID**:

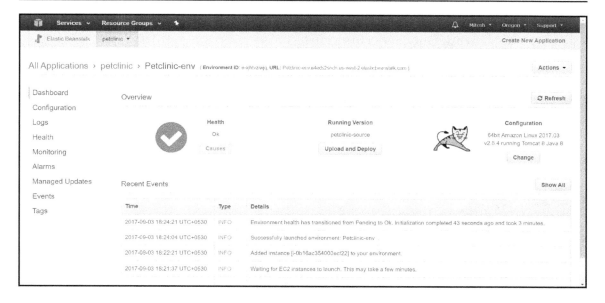

Our sample application is ready. It is hosted in an AWS Elastic Beanstalk that has created an instance in the public subnet of our `packt` VPC.

5. Go to **Configuration** and verify the software configuration and other configurations as well:

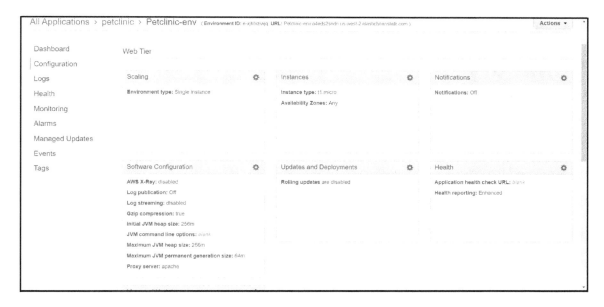

The monitoring section provides data for CPU utilization, as well as **Network In** and **Network Out** data in the portal.

6. Click on **Environments**; a green box signals that the environment is healthy:

We have now created a VPC and hosted an instance in it by using AWS Elastic Beanstalk.

Summary

We are at the end of this chapter, so let's summarize what we have covered.

We have covered two ways to create a virtual private cloud: one with the wizard and one without it. Of course, creating a VPC with the wizard is quicker and easier, but it is more desirable to work with a custom VPC first so that we know what is going on behind the scenes when we create a VPC with the wizard.

Once we had created a custom VPC, we created an application in Elastic Beanstalk that is a PaaS offering from AWS. We then created an environment in the application and deployed a sample application in the environment. While creating and configuring the application and environment, we configured our custom VPC for launching instances; hence, all the instances that were created in the PaaS will be created in the custom VPC.

The user should delete the VPC in order to avoid unnecessary costs. Deleting NAT gateways might take a while, which will abort the deletion of the VPC. After the NAT gateway is deleted, you can try to delete the VPC again. It is important to note here that the EIP addresses are not released; these need to be deleted as well.

In the next chapter, we will provide an overview of the **Elastic Load Balancer** and how to create and configure it.

Elastic Load Balancing 3

High availability and fault-tolerance are essential features of any modern day application. It is necessary to distribute the load and to avoid single points of failure when it comes to application access.

AWS-provided **Elastic Load Balancing** (**ELB**) automatically distributes incoming traffic to different instances that are launched in different availability zones.

AWS Elastic Load Balancing provides the following three types of load balancer:

- Application Load Balancer
- Network Load Balancer
- Classic Load Balancer

In this chapter, we will focus on Application Load Balancer in detail with the use of a sample application. We will also see how Elastic Load Balancing automatically distributes incoming application traffic across multiple Amazon EC2 instances in the cloud to achieve higher levels of fault-tolerance in the application. We will explore the following topics:

- An overview of ELB
- Creating and configuring ELB

An overview of ELB

Consider a scenario where you want to distribute traffic to multiple instances, maybe in different availability zones or different regions, in order to configure high availability and fault-tolerance. AWS Elastic Load Balancing provides the following three types of load balancers:

- **Application Load Balancer**: Works at Layer 7 and routes HTTP and HTTPS traffic to EC2 instances, IP addresses, and containers. It is mandatory to specify more than one Availability Zone. Having the capacity to route traffic in multiple Availability Zones and scaling the request-handling capacity automatically provides natural support for high availability.
- **Network Load Balancer**: Works at Layer 4 and routes TCP traffic to EC2 instances, IP addresses, and containers. It allows incoming traffic and distributes it across targets within the same Availability Zone with the capability to suddenly volatile traffic patterns and extremely low latencies. Network Load Balancer allows one static IP per Availability Zone and one Elastic IP per Availability Zone.
- **Classic Load Balancer**: Provides basic load balancing across EC2 instances, IP addresses, and containers within the EC2-Classic network. It allows incoming traffic and distributes it within a single Availability Zone or multiple Availability Zones.

 You should choose a load balancer based on the needs of an application. A detailed comparison of Application Load Balancer, Network Load Balancer, and Classic Load Balancer is available at `https://aws.amazon.com/elasticloadbalancing/details`.

In Application Load Balancer, Network Load Balancer, and Classic Load Balancer, you are billed for each hour or partial hour that a specific load balancer is running. In Application Load Balancer and Network Load Balancer, billing is done based on the number of **Load Balancer Capacity Units** (**LCUs**) that are used per hour. In the case of Classic Load Balancer, it is based on each GB of data that's transferred through your Classic Load Balancer.

 For more details on Elastic Load Balancing Pricing, visit `https://aws.amazon.com/elasticloadbalancing/pricing/`.

In the next section, we will cover how to create an Application Load Balancer.

Creating and configuring an ELB

We are going to create instances in a default VPC, and then we will configure the load balancer to route the traffic to instances.

Let's create an instance in the free tier, then install Tomcat and deploy an application in it:

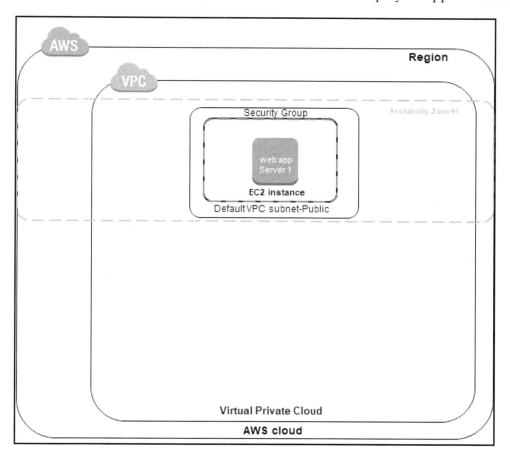

1. Go to **Services** | **Compute** | **EC2** | **Instances** | **Launch Instance**:

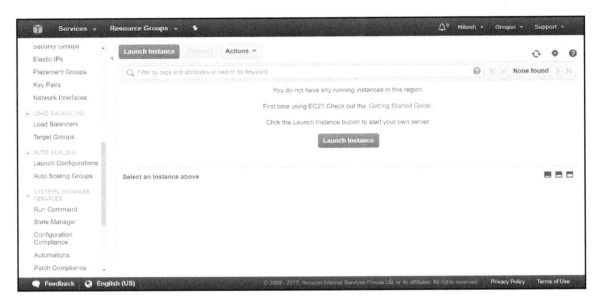

2. Select **Amazon Linux AMI**. Keep the instance type as **t2.micro**:

3. Click on **Next: Configure Instance Details**.
4. Select the default VPC and subnet to launch the instance. Click on **Next: Add Storage**:

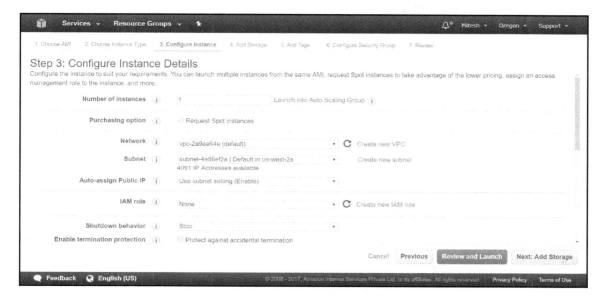

5. Keep the default settings and select **Next: Add Tags**.
6. Add tags if required and click on **Next: Configure Security Group**.

7. Select the default security group or create a new security group. Click on **Review and Launch**:

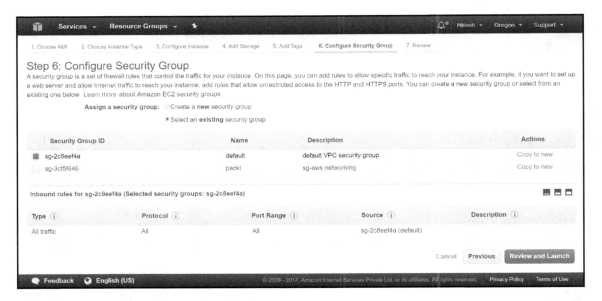

8. Review all the configured details and click on **Launch**.
9. Select the key-pair available to you so that you can access the instance remotely, create a runtime environment, and deploy an application:

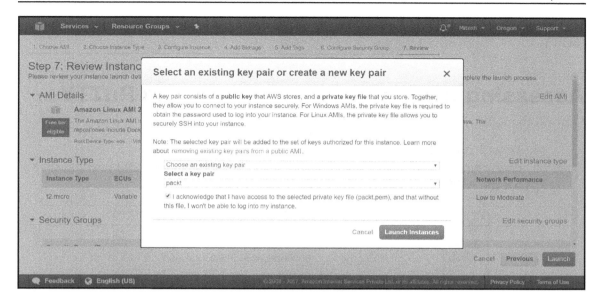

10. You will see your instance being launched. Go to the **Instances** section of the **EC2 Dashboard**.

11. The instance will be initializing. Note the public IP address and public DNS:

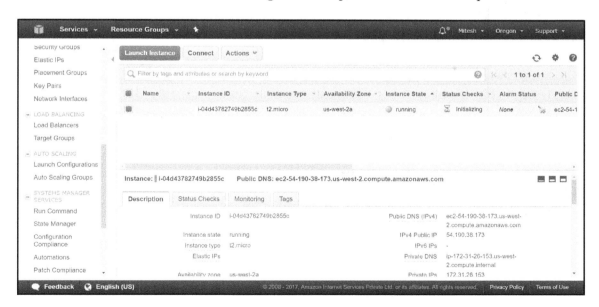

The status check is complete. Let's try to access the instance remotely with the use of PuTTY.

Accessing the instance remotely using PuTTY

Perform the following steps to access the instance remotely:

1. Download PuTTY.
2. Open **PuTTY Configuration** and provide a public IP address and port number for the AWS instance to remotely access the instance:

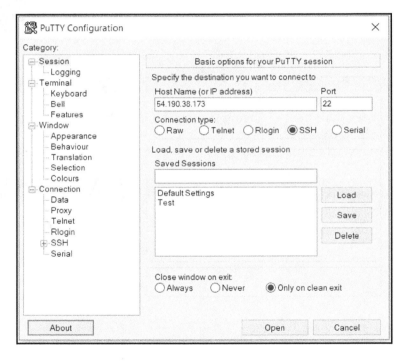

3. Go to **Connection** | **SSH** | **Auth**.
4. Provide the PPK file in the **Private key file for authentication** field:

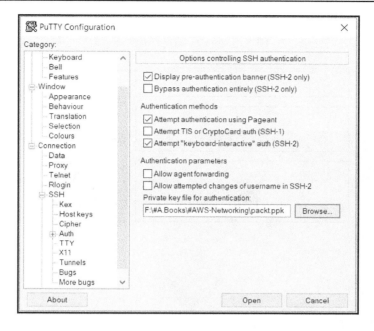

5. Click on **Open**. Access to the instance won't be available. In this case, go to the security group that has been configured for the instance and open the SSH rule in inbound rules so that your machine can access it:

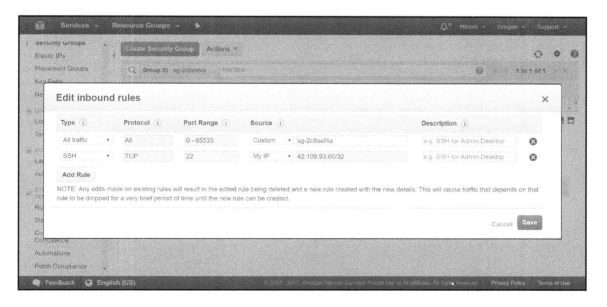

6. Try to open remote access using PuTTY.
7. Click on **Yes** in the **PuTTY Security Alert** screen:

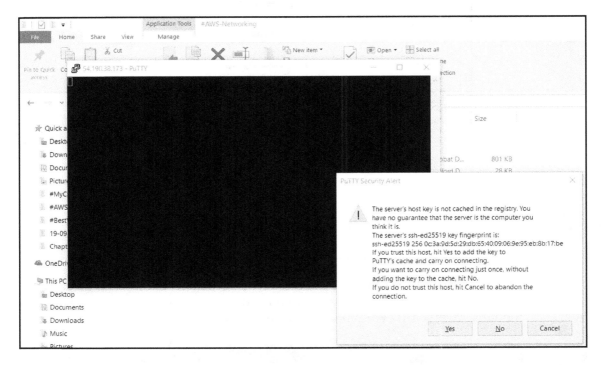

Once we are able to access the instance remotely, let's install Tomcat so that we can deploy the sample WAR file:

1. Go to `https://tomcat.apache.org/download-80.cgi`.
2. Copy the download link for Tomcat 8.
3. Go to PuTTY, where we have been connected to the AWS instance.
4. Execute
   `wget http://www-eu.apache.org/dist/tomcat/tomcat-8/v8.5.20/bin/`
   `apache-tomcat-8.5.20.tar.gz`.

5. Once the download is successful, extract the files using the `tar zxpvf apache-tomcat-8.5.20.tar.gz` command:

6. Go to the `TOMCAT/bin` directory and start Tomcat by executing the `./startup.sh` command in PuTTY:

7. Try to access the Tomcat instance using the default port, 8080. We won't be able to access Tomcat as the security group does not allow it. Let's configure port 8080 for access.

8. Go to Amazon's **EC2 Dashboard | Security Groups** and select the default security group. Then, click on **Edit** in the **Inbound** tab:

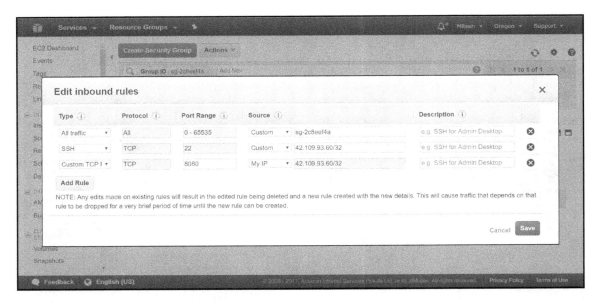

9. Try to access the Tomcat instance with your public DNS and default port 8080:

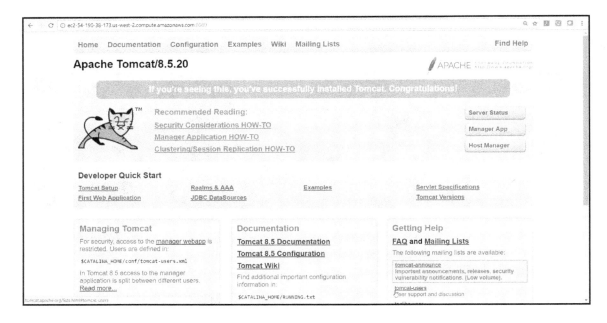

10. Use WinSCP and transfer any working WAR file to the remote instance. In our case, we transferred `petclinic.war`.

11. Let's create another instance in a different Availability Zone. Install Tomcat and deploy the same application:

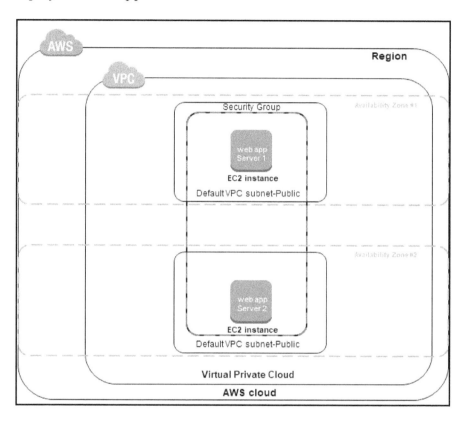

12. Verify access to the application using your public DNS and the default port number:

Now, we will create an ELB and configure target groups to which traffic will be routed using ELB:

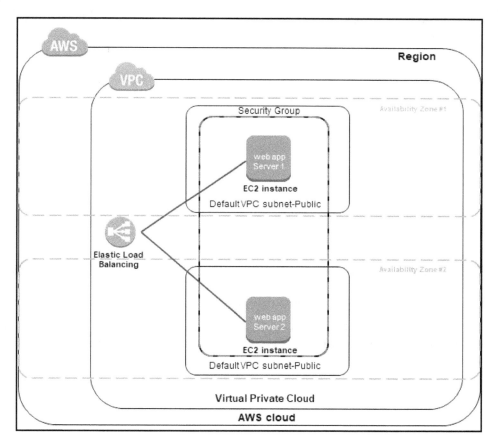

1. Go to **EC2 Dashboard** | **LOAD BALANCING** | **Load Balancers**.
2. Click on **Create Load Balancer**.

3. Click on **Create** under **Application Load Balancer**:

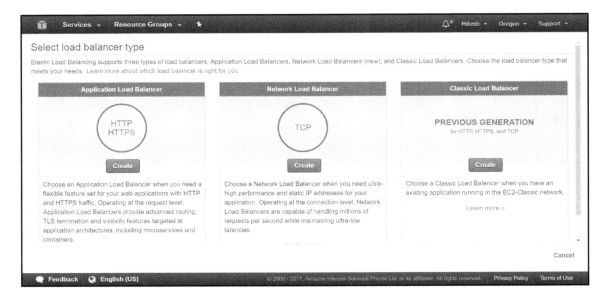

4. In the **Configure Load Balancer** step, provide the **Name**, **Scheme**, and **Listeners**:

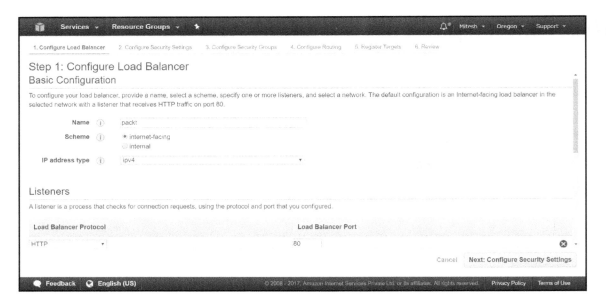

5. Configure two subnets from two different Availability Zones:

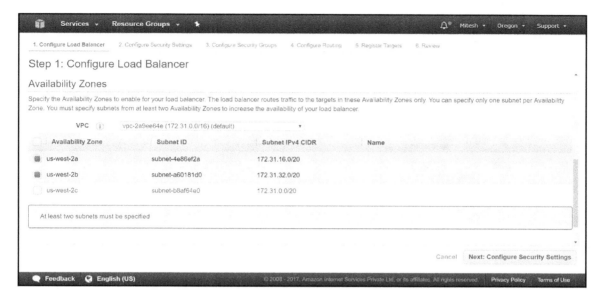

6. Click on **Next: Configure Security Settings**:

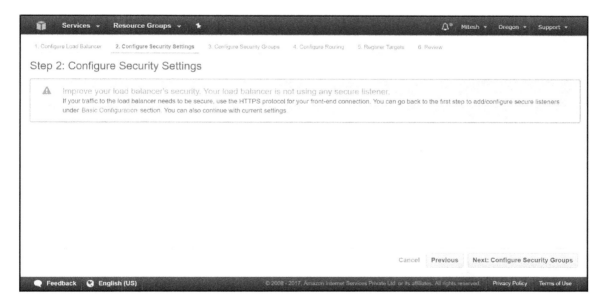

7. Select the default security group or create a new security group specifically for ELB.

8. Click on **Next: Configure Routing**.

9. Let's **Configure Routing** with **Target Group** and **Health checks**.

10. Allocate **Port** 8080 since the instances will listen on port 8080.

11. Select **Protocol** and **Path**. If Path is not working, we may need to change it so that healthy targets are ready to listen.

12. Click on **Next: Register Targets**:

13. Select instances and click on **Add to registered** by selecting port `8080`:

14. Click on **Next: Review** and then click on **Create**.

15. Verify the load balancer's creation status. You have successfully created a load balancer!

16. Go to the **EC2 Dashboard** and check out the newly created load balancer. Note the **DNS name**. The load balancer is still in the **provisioning** state:

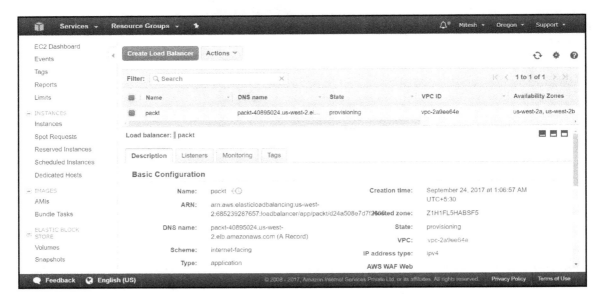

17. Wait until the load balancer is in the **active** state:

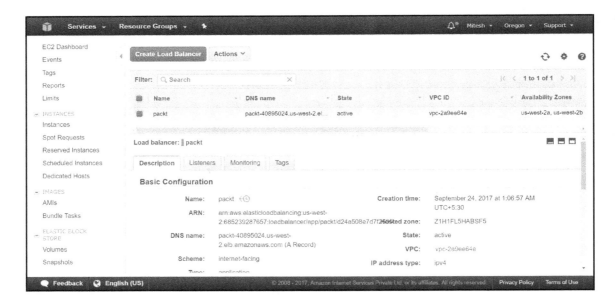

18. Click on the **Listeners** tab and verify the added listener:

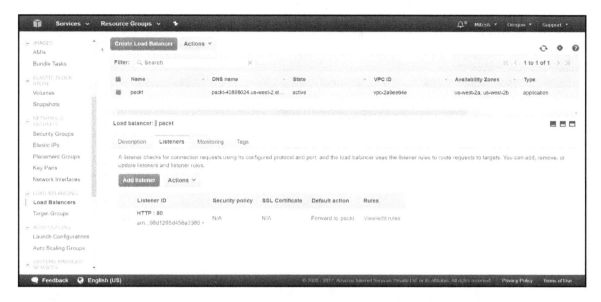

19. The **Monitoring** tab provides CloudWatch metrics.
20. Go to **Target Groups**.

21. Go to the **Targets** tab to review **Registered targets** and the status of the instances. All the instances have to be in a **healthy** state:

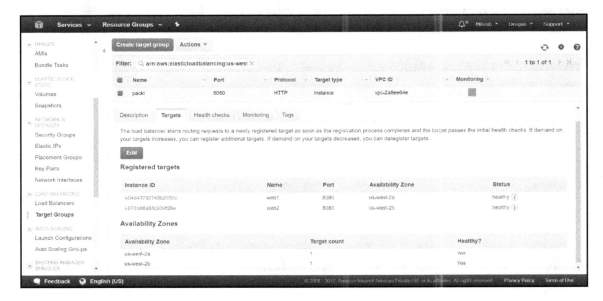

22. The **Description** tab contains basic configuration and attributes.
23. The **Health checks** tab contains data related to the path, protocol, port, threshold, timeout, interval, and success code.
24. We changed our path here as the earlier path was not detected and hence the instance state was unhealthy:

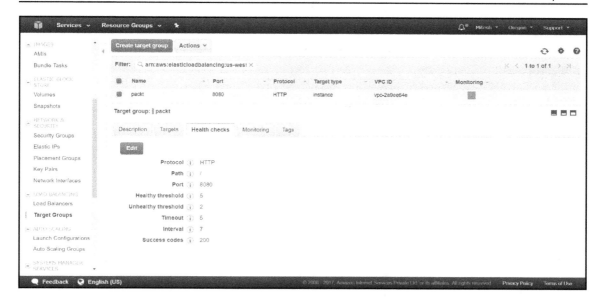

Now, we are ready to access the instances using the ELB DNS name:

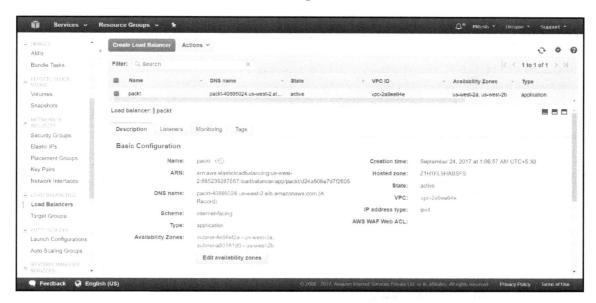

We are going to achieve the following scenario:

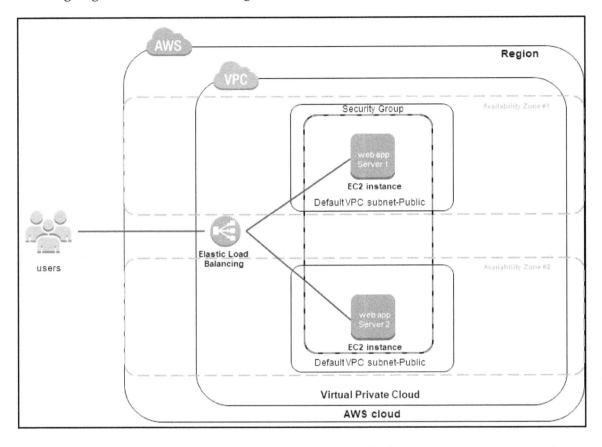

1. Go to **Security Groups** and add an Inbound rule for port 80 since we are going to use it instead of port 80. Remove the rule related to port 8080 since we are only going to access the application using ELB.
2. Use the ELB DNS name and try to access the application. We changed the welcome message in the second instance so that we know where the requests are going.

   AWS does not expose the public IP address of the ELB and forces the user to use the DNS name.

3. Try to hit the ELB DNS name multiple times, and you will get a response from another instance too.

We have successfully configured ELB for two different instances in two different Availability Zones, and it worked for a sample application.

Summary

Well done! We are at the end of this chapter, so let's summarize what we have covered.

We created two instances in two different Availability Zones in the default VPC. We installed Tomcat by accessing instances with the use of PuTTY. Using WinSCP, we transferred a sample application in the Tomcat installation directory for deployment. Then, we created a load balancer and configured target groups.

Once ELB and the target groups were configured properly, we accessed our sample application using the ELB DNS name rather than using it with the public DNS name of instances.

In the next chapter, we will look at auto-scaling in detail.

Auto Scaling 4

In this chapter, we will focus on how to configure instances in VPC for Auto Scaling, and consider what and how to configure to make our application highly available.

It is important to understand what exactly scaling is! In this chapter, we will cover vertical scaling and horizontal scaling in detail.

After understanding the basics of scaling and the different types of scaling, we will create an instance in the default VPC, install a runtime environment, and deploy a sample application.

Once the instance is ready, we will create an **Amazon Machine Image (AMI)** out of it, which we will use while creating an Auto Scaling group.

Once the AMI is ready, we will create an Auto Scaling group. However, we need to launch the configuration we've created before we can create it.

We will cover the following topics in this chapter:

- An overview of Auto Scaling
- Vertical and horizontal scaling
- Setting up Auto Scaling in a load balanced application

An overview of Auto Scaling

It's possible that you may need to adjust the number of resources that are serving the application so that application load can be managed without any issues. The manual configuration of increasing and decreasing resources based on application load faces many difficulties, and hardly serves its purpose effectively.

It is better to scale in and scale out automatically so that whenever a peak load is encountered by the application, additional resources can be allocated automatically. Then, when the load is back to normal, additional resources can be deallocated.

There are some visible benefits of Auto Scaling, as shown in the following diagram:

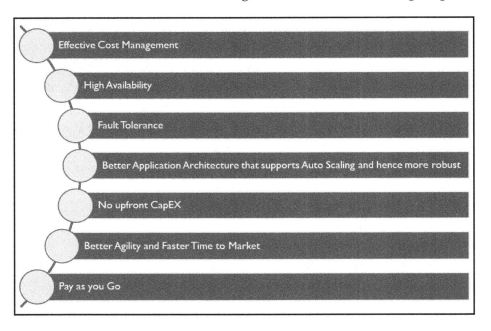

In short, the Auto Scaling feature in AWS provides us with the flexibility to manage application traffic in a cost-effective manner. We can achieve this by configuring the minimum number of instances in each Auto Scaling group. This minimum number of instances in each Auto Scaling group configuration ensures that all of the instances that are available to serve traffic are equal to the configuration. Similarly, we can also configure the maximum number of instances in each Auto Scaling group. This configuration ensures that the number of instances serving the application traffic doesn't go beyond the maximum number of instances.

Types of Auto Scaling

Before we configure Auto Scaling in AWS, let's look at some popular scaling types that are used on a daily basis.

There are two types of scaling:

- **Horizontal scaling (scale in and scale out)**: Horizontal scaling is all about adding new resources to manage the application load. Consider a scenario where an e-commerce site has announced a sale in a festival season. The web application gets many requests in such a scenario for a specific duration of time.

    In this case, we can add multiple instances or resources, each with a similar configuration, so that they all try to serve requests in a better way:

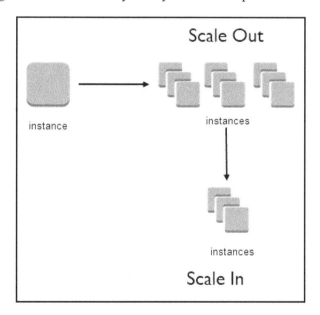

    However, in such a scenario, the application architecture needs to support (stateless) situations where multiple instances are added, and where instances are removed when the load is normal.

- **Vertical scaling (scale up and scale down)**: Vertical scaling is all about increasing and decreasing the capacity of a single resource or an instance:

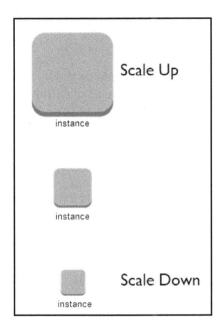

For example, increasing RAM or hard disk space based on certain requirements is something that we often find very common in traditional environments. Nowadays, scaling down is rarely performed by organizations.

In the next section, we will set up Auto Scaling in AWS.

Setting up Auto Scaling in a load balanced application

Let's look at the process of creating an Auto Scaling group in AWS, step by step.

The objective is to create the following architecture using the Auto Scaling group:

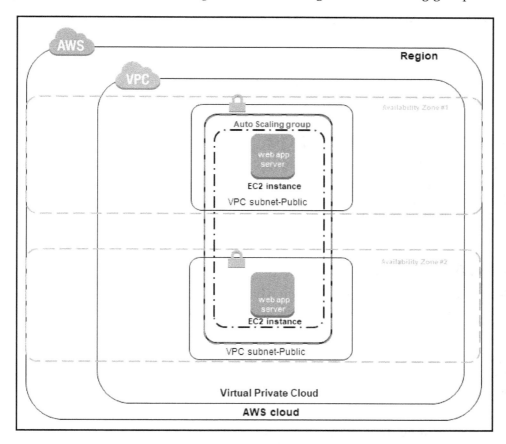

The following diagram shows the steps for the rest of the sections in this chapter:

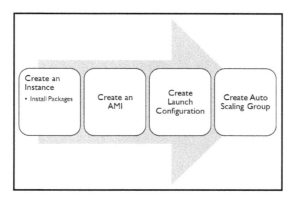

There are three major components of Auto Scaling in AWS:

- **Amazon Machine Image** (**AMI**)
- Launch configuration
- Auto Scaling group

Now, let's cover each of these components.

Amazon Machine Image

An **Amazon Machine Image** (**AMI**) is a template where we have already installed all the necessary packages and deployed the application package to a web server. Here, a Spring-based application needs to be deployed, so AMI will need to have Java and Tomcat installed in the application package.

Launch configuration

This is a template that provides details on which type of instances need to be launched in the Auto Scaling group. You can select the type of instance, select a custom AMI, or select an AMI from the Marketplace.

 Only 100 launch configurations per region are allowed.

At the time of creating the Auto Scaling group, you need the launch configuration available. If it is not available, then you will be asked to create one. Then, Auto Scaling group creation will start.

 You can only launch one configuration for an Auto Scaling group at a time.

Auto Scaling group

An Auto Scaling group is a collection of similar instances that are logically united. Consider a scenario where you need to deploy a Spring-based application. The instance must have Java and Tomcat installed. There must be specific requirements related to the capacity of the instances as well.

In such a scenario, an Auto Scaling group will have all the instances that have Java and Tomcat installed—plus the application that's been deployed in Tomcat—and running successfully.

The following two operations are possible in an Auto Scaling group:

- Increase the number of instances to manage a high volume of requests
- Decrease the number of instances to manage costs when the volume of requests is not that high

Only 20 Auto Scaling groups per region is allowed.

Now, the important question is, how does an Auto Scaling group know which kind of instances with which packages need to be launched when the volume of requests is very high?

For this, we need to use an AMI that has everything configured and the application deployed as well.

There is no additional cost associated with the Auto Scaling feature in AWS.

Let's create an AMI first:

1. Go to **Services** | **Compute**. Click on **EC2, Instances**, and then **Launch Instance.**
2. Select the **Amazon Linux AMI:**

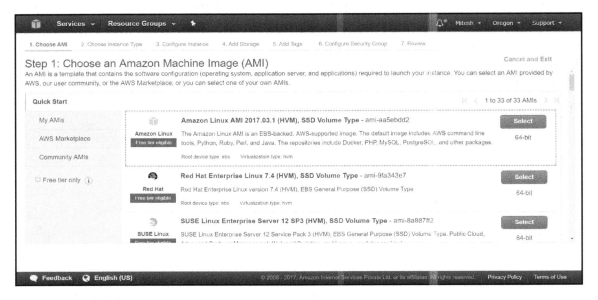

3. Keep the instance type as `t2.micro`.
4. Click on the **Configure Instance** details.
5. Select the default VPC and subnet to launch the instance.
6. Click on **Add Storage**.
7. Select the default security group or create a new security group.
8. Click on **Review** and **Launch**.
9. Review all the configured details and click on **Launch:**

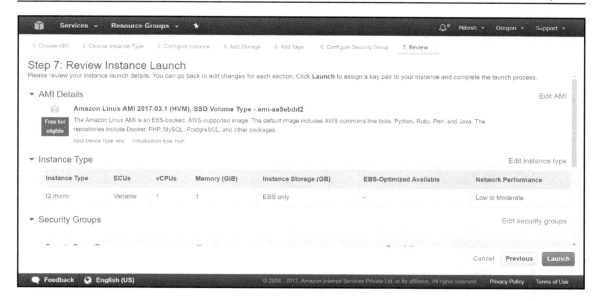

10. Select the key pair that's available so that you can access the instance remotely, create a runtime environment, and deploy an application.

The instance should be launching. Go to the **Instances** section of the EC2 dashboard.

The instance is now in the initializing state. Note the public IP address and public DNS:

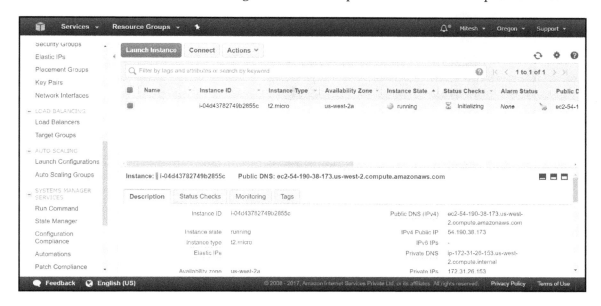

After a few minutes, the status check will complete. Now, try to access the instance remotely with the use of PuTTY:

1. Open **PuTTY Configuration** and provide the public IP address and port number to remotely access the instance.
2. Go to **Connection | SSH | Auth**.
3. Provide the PPK file in the field named **Private key file for authentication**:

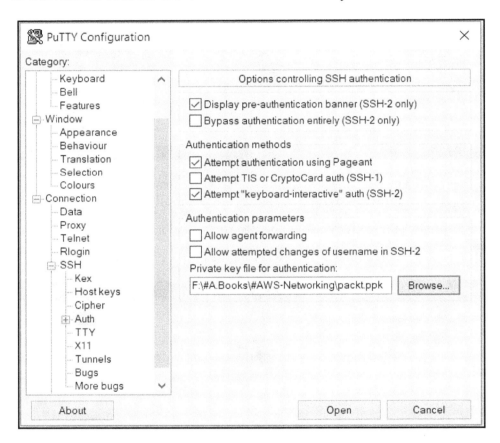

4. Click on **Open**. Instance access won't be available. In this case, go to the security group that's been configured for the instance and open **SSH rule** in **Edit inbound rules** so that your machine can access it:

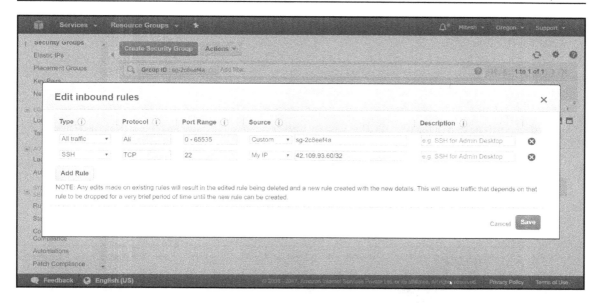

5. Try to open remote access using PuTTY again.
6. Click on **Yes** in the **PuTTY Security Alert** that appears:

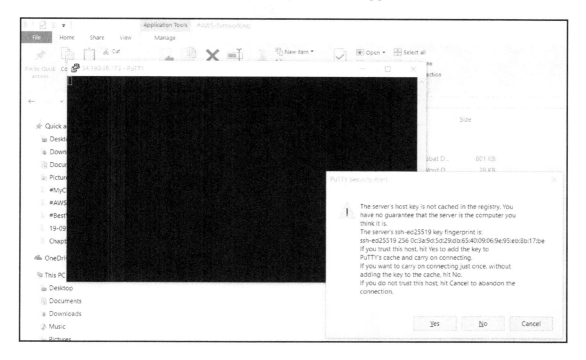

Now that we can access the instance remotely, let's install Tomcat so that we can deploy a sample WAR file:

1. Go to `https://tomcat.apache.org/download-80.cgi`.
2. Copy the download link for Tomcat 8.
3. Go to PuTTY, where we have now been connected to the AWS instance.
4. Upon execution, we get the following link: `http://www-eu.apache.org/dist/tomcat/tomcat-8/v8.5.20/bin/apache-tomcat-8.5.20.tar.gz`.
5. Once the download is successful, extract the files using the `tar zxpvf apache-tomcat-8.5.20.tar.gz` command.
6. Go to the `TOMCAT/bin` directory and start `tomcat` by executing the `./startup.sh` command in PuTTY:

7. Try to access the Tomcat instance using default port `8080`. We won't be able to access Tomcat as the security group won't allow this:

Now, let's configure port `8080` for access:

1. Go to Amazon **EC2 Dashboard** | **Security Groups**, select the default security group, and click on **Edit inbound rules**:

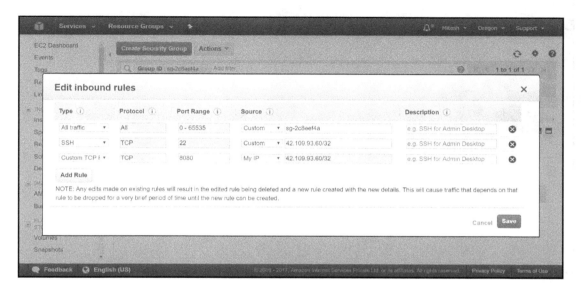

2. Now, access the Tomcat instance with your public DNS and default port `8080`:

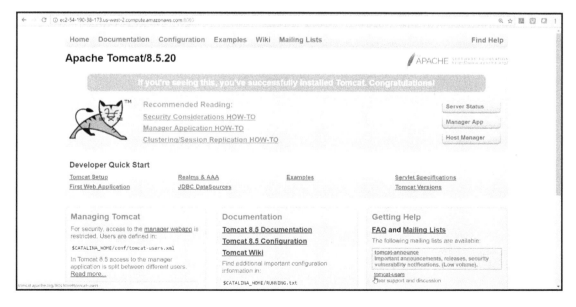

3. Use WinSCP and transfer any working WAR file to the remote instance. In our case, we have transferred `petclinic.war`:

Now, the instance is ready and the application has been deployed inside it.

4. Select an instance.
5. Right-click on the instance, select **Image**, and click on **Create Image**:

6. Give the image a name and description.
7. Click on **Create Image**.
8. Click on **Close**.
9. In the left sidebar, go to **IMAGES AMIs**. Wait for the image to be created. Once the image is available, its status will change to available:

Now, let's manage some EC2 instances automatically:

1. In **EC2 Dashboard**, go to the left sidebar, select **AUTOSCALING**, and then select **Auto Scaling Group**.
2. Select **Create Auto Scaling group**:

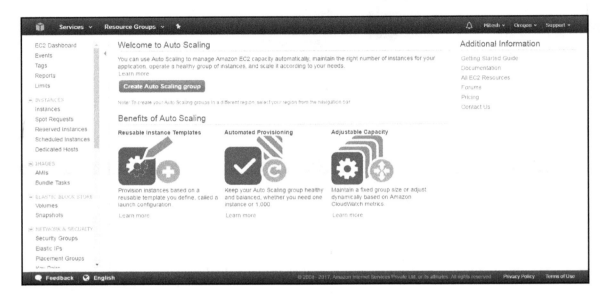

In our scenario, no launch configuration is available, which is why we're first prompted to create a launch configuration before creating an Auto Scaling group.

3. Click on **Create launch configuration**.
4. On the **Choose AMI** page, select AMI:

5. Once the AMI has been selected, select the **Instance type**:

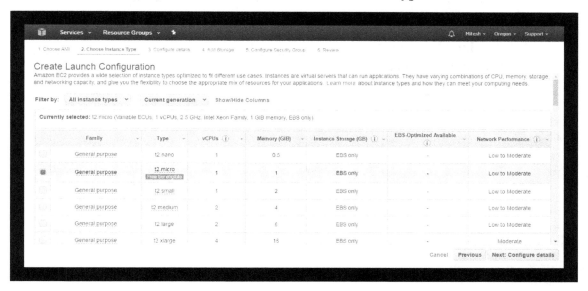

6. Select `t2.micro` as it is free tier eligible.

7. Click on **Configure details**:

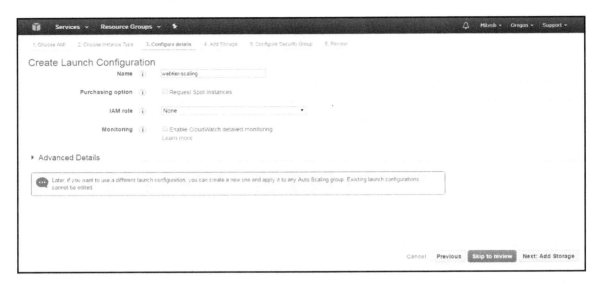

8. Provide a name for the launch configuration.
9. Select **Enable CloudWatch detailed monitoring**.
10. Click on **Add Storage**:

11. Keep the default configuration. Click on **Configure Security Group**.
12. Create a new security group or configure an existing security group.

13. Click on **Review**:

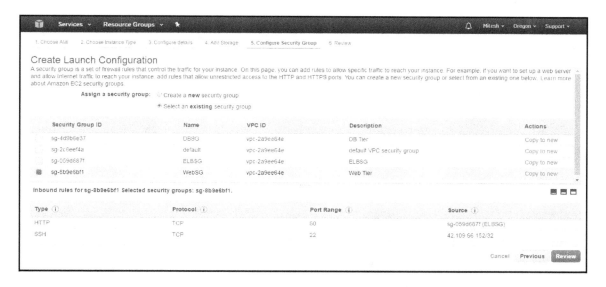

14. On the **Review** page, verify all the details and click on **Create launch configuration**:

15. Here, you can either select an existing key pair or create a new key pair. Select an existing key pair.

16. Select the acknowledgement checkbox and then click on **Create launch configuration**:

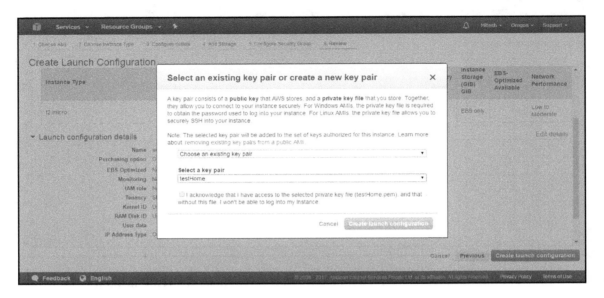

Once the launch configuration is available, it is time to configure the Auto Scaling group:

1. On the configure **Auto Scaling Group** page, give a **Group name** and a **Group size** that describes the number of instances for the Auto Scaling group initially. In this case, we want 2 instances to start with, so 2 instances is given.

2. In **Network**, select any custom VPC or default VPC that you can create instances in. Launch your instance in an Amazon VPC. This will give you complete control over your virtual networking environment. You can select your own IP address range, create subnets, configure route tables, and configure network gateways here as well.

3. Select the subnets that will host an instance. These subnets are available in the VPC that you selected in the previous step. A range of IP addresses in your VPC that can be used to isolate different EC2 resources from each other or from the internet can be found here.

4. To use a public subnet in your instance, you must be connected to the internet or a private subnet. Subnets also provide an additional layer of security, including security groups and a network **Access Control List** (**ACL**).

5. Select two subnets of the three that are available for our scenario:

6. Click on **Advanced Details** to configure more of their details, such as **Load Balancer**, **Health Check Grace Period**, and **Monitoring**:

7. Click on **Configure scaling policies**. On the **Configure scaling policies** page, there are two options:
    - **Keep this group at its initial size**: This allows you to adjust the size of an Auto Scaling group manually based on requirements
    - **Use scaling policies to adjust the capacity of this group**: This allows you to configure scenarios where the size of the Auto Scaling group is automatically adjusted based on criteria that you specify

 Only 50 scaling policies per Auto Scaling group are allowed.

8. Now, click on **Configure Notifications**. You can configure the notification settings so that you get an email whenever the instance is launched successfully, apply instance termination, and also look at failed instance terminations:

9. Click on **Review**:

On the **Review** page, verify the details that we have configured up until now.

10. Click on **Create Auto Scaling group**. AWS portal will provide the status of the Auto Scaling group's creation.

11. Click on **Close**.

12. In the AWS portal, go to **Auto Scaling Groups** and verify the configuration that we have completed:

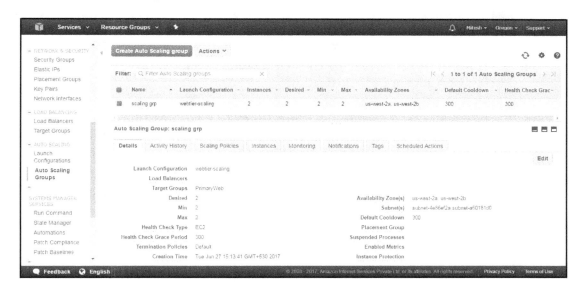

Since we have kept it at a minimum size, that is, **2**, observe the number of instances in the **EC2 Dashboard**. Another instance will be created.

Let's try and select **Use scaling policies to adjust the capacity of this group** and look at the difference between the two configurations.

Here, you can configure the number of instances and metric types for automatic scaling:

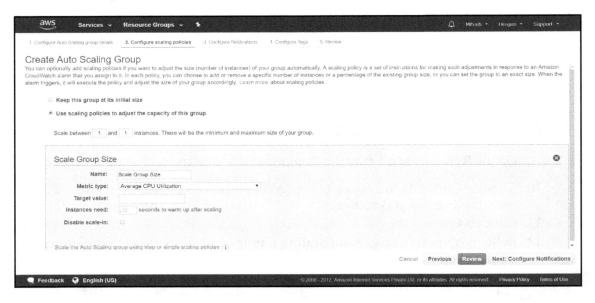

13. Configure instances from 1 to 3 in the scale between instances.
14. Select **Metric type** as **Average CPU Utilization**. In this case, we want to keep it as 75 percent **Average CPU Utilization**.
15. Click on **Configure Notification** or **Review**.
16. Review all the configurations and click on **Create Auto Scaling group**:

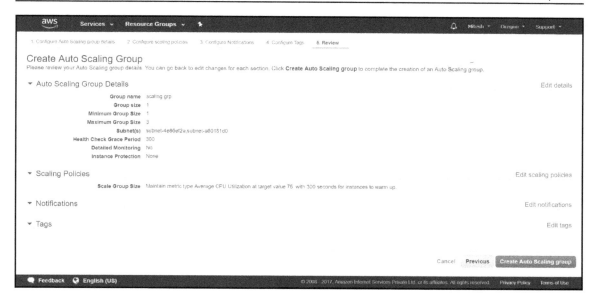

Just to verify whether our Auto Scaling policy is working or not, try to terminate the instance, and within a few seconds, a new instance will be created immediately.

Auto Scaling provides a lot of flexibility at no additional cost. Yes, that's right. You are charged for the instances that are created during the scaling operation and not for using Auto Scaling services.

Summary

Well done! We have come to the end of this chapter, so let's summarize what we have covered.

In this chapter, you understood the concept of scaling and types of scaling, such as vertical and horizontal. We created an Auto Scaling group, and configured manual and automated scaling while creating it.

In the next chapter, we will cover Amazon Route 53 concepts and understand private addresses and Elastic IP addresses.

Amazon Route 53 5

In this chapter, we will focus on using Amazon Route 53 for domain names and routing traffic to resources for a domain.

Amazon Route 53 is a domain name system (or DNS) service. It is a reliable and scalable service that has DNS servers distributed globally. It scales automatically to manage spikes in DNS queries, and so it is robust.

The pricing model of Amazon Route 53 is pay as you go. We can purchase a domain name from Route 53 or we can transfer it from an existing provider. We can also utilize Route 53 as a DNS service only.

First, we need to create a hosted zone. Each hosted zone requires a record set that provides mapping to the IP address or CNAME with the domain name.

This chapter will cover the following topics:

- Overview of Amazon Route 53 concepts
- Configuring Amazon Route 53
- Configuring Route 53 for a web application

Overview of Amazon Route 53 concepts

Amazon Route 53 provides a facility to register domain names—also called a **domain name system** (**DNS**) service—so that domain names are translated into IP addresses, and also supplies health checks by sending automated requests to the application for updates on its availability. The main page of Amazon Route 53 is shown in the following screenshot:

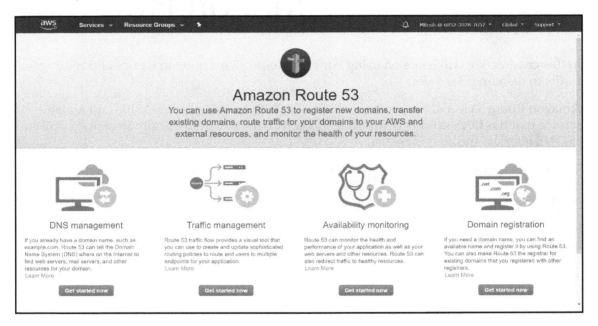

For your website to have a global reach and brand value, it should have a name. This is the domain name that users use to visit your website. Amazon Route 53 provides the facility to register domain names. There are situations where you must have purchased the domain name from other providers; in such cases, you can optionally transfer it to Amazon Route 53. Amazon Route 53 uses CloudWatch alarms to monitor the health of resources, such as web servers and email servers.

Configuring Amazon Route 53

In this section, we will configure Route 53. We will also demonstrate the process of domain registration.

To configure Amazon Route 53, follow these steps:

1. Go to **Services** | **Networking & Content Delivery** | **Route 53**.
2. Click on **Get started now** for **Domain registration**, as shown in the following screenshot:

3. Click on **Register Domain**, as shown in the following screenshot:

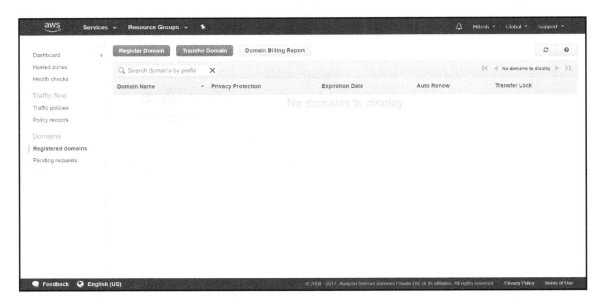

4. Enter the domain name that you want to register and then click on **Check**, as shown in the following screenshot:

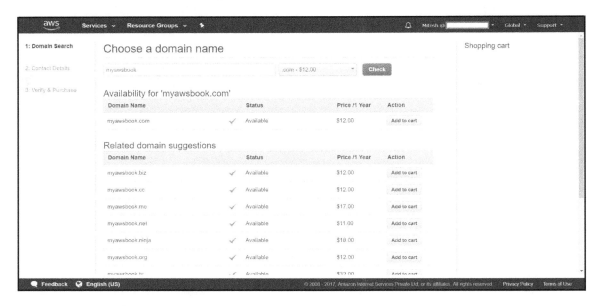

5. Click on **Add to Cart** for a suitable and available domain name. Click on **Continue**.

6. Select the number of years in the **Register in the Year** field.

7. Provide your contact details.

8. You can also configure privacy protection. This governs whether you want to conceal your contact information from WHOIS queries. If you select **Yes**, your contact information will be masked. If you select **No**, your contact information will be publicly available.

9. Click on **Continue**.

10. Verify and purchase the domain name.

Configuring Route 53 for a web application

Before configuring Route 53 for the sample web application that's been deployed in the Amazon Elastic Beanstalk, let's look at what a public hosted zone is. A public hosted zone contains information about routing traffic for a domain and its subdomains. Basically, it responds to queries based on the resource record set that's created by a user. It is important to understand that once you create the public hosted zone, a **name server** (**NS**) record and a **start of authority** (**SOA**) record are automatically created. The NS record is important here. It provides you with four name servers that you need to configure with your registrar or DNS services so that all the queries related to your domain are routed to Amazon Route 53 name servers for resolution.

To set up a hosted zone, go through the following steps:

 If we purchase a domain from Route 53, then the hosted zone is created automatically and we don't need to create one.

1. Sign in to the AWS Management Console.

2. Go to the Amazon Route 53 dashboard from the **Services** menu or visit `https://console.aws.amazon.com/route53/`.

3. On the left sidebar, spot the **Hosted zones**. As of now, there is no **Hosted zone** available.

4. Click on **Create Hosted Zone**, as shown in the following screenshot:

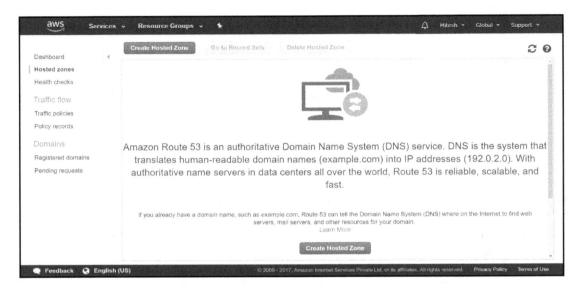

5. In the **Create Hosted Zone** section, provide the **Domain Name**, **Comments**, and **Type**.
6. Click on **Create**. As we mentioned earlier, four name servers are associated with the public hosted zone, as shown in the following screenshot:

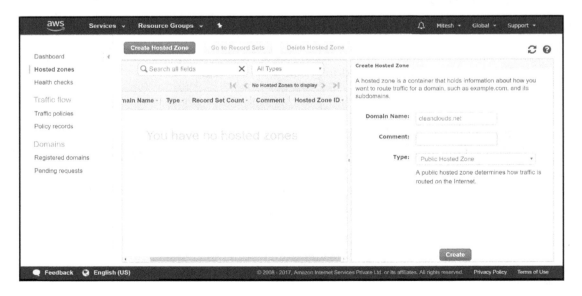

7. Select a public hosted zone and verify the details, including the TTL in seconds and the name server values, as shown in the following screenshot:

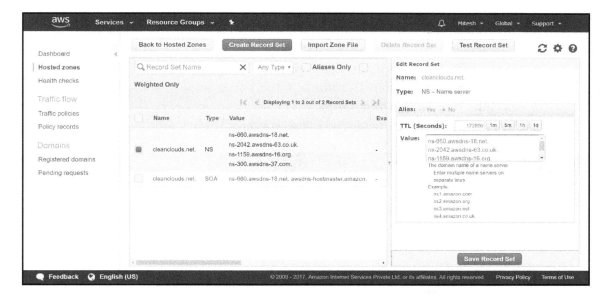

To add and update name servers with a registered domain, follow these steps:

1. Note down all four of the name server values available with the hosted zone. We need to use these name server values in our registered domain.
2. Click on **Registered domains** and select the domain that you have already purchased.
3. Click on the **Domain name**.
4. Click on **Add/Edit Name Servers**.
5. Update the **Name Servers**.
6. Click on **Update**.

Now, the public hosted zone is available.

Let's consider a scenario where the application is hosted in an Amazon EC2 instance and we want to route traffic to an Amazon EC2 instance. The following steps demonstrate this process:

1. Create an Amazon EC2 instance and note down its public IP address.
2. In the record set, provide www as the name.
3. Select an IPv4 address in the **Type** field.
4. Give the instance's public IP address in the **Value** field.
5. Select the **Simple Routing Policy.**
6. Click on **Create**, as shown in the following screenshot:

Configuring health checks on Route 53

Let's look at how health checks can be configured on Route 53 by going through the following steps:

1. Click on **Health checks**.
2. Click on **Create health check**, as shown in the following screenshot:

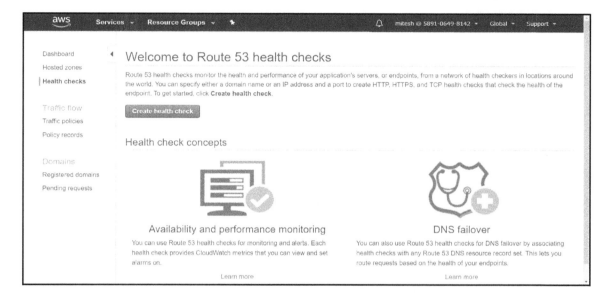

3. Give a **Name** to the health check. Select an endpoint in the **What to Monitor** section.
4. Select **Specify endpoint by** IP address.

5. Provide the IP address of the EC2 instance that you want to monitor. Provide a port number, as per your requirements:

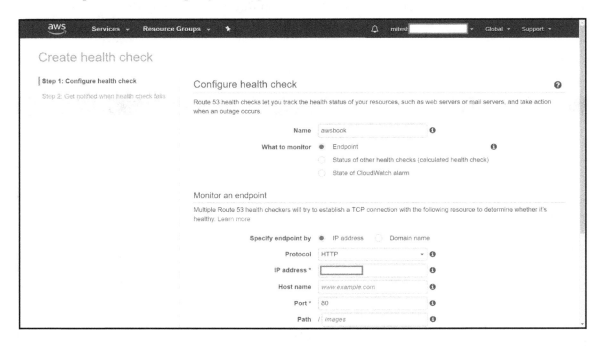

6. To get notifications when a health check fails, select **Create alarm**.
7. Select **New SNS topic** from the **Send notification to** dropdown.
8. Provide a **Topic name** and recipients.

9. Click on **Create health check**, as shown in the following screenshot:

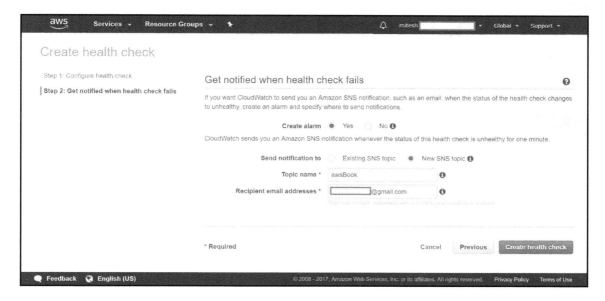

10. Wait for some time and you will get the status of the EC2 instance, as shown in the following screenshot:

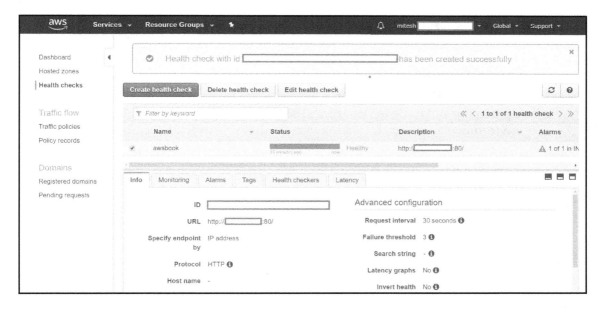

Now, let's focus on deploying the application in AWS Elastic Beanstalk by going through the following steps:

1. Go to the **Services** menu and select **AWS Elastic Beanstalk**.
2. Create a new application.
3. Once the application is available, create a new environment.
4. Check the availability of the domain name, as shown in the following screenshot:

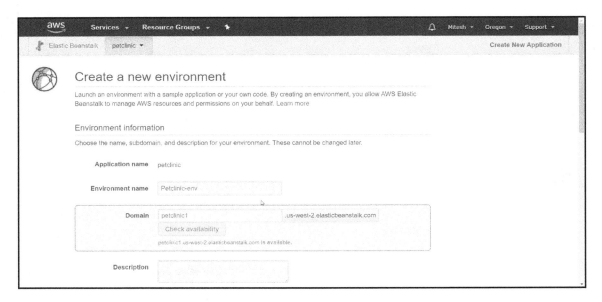

5. Provide **Platform** details.
6. Provide the **Application Code**.
7. Upload the WAR file to Amazon S3 so that it can be directly utilized in any of the environments, or use an existing version that was uploaded earlier.

8. Click on **Create environment**, as shown in the following screenshot:

9. Verify the execution of the **AWS Elastic Beanstalk** in the dashboard. It will create a security group, an Elastic IP address, and then the environment, as shown in the following screenshot:

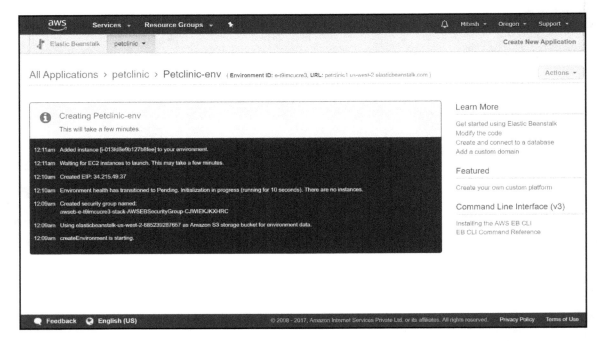

10. Once the environment has been created and the application has been deployed successfully, go to the environment dashboard. Verify the health of the application environment, the application version, and the configuration of the EC2 instance, as shown in the following screenshot:

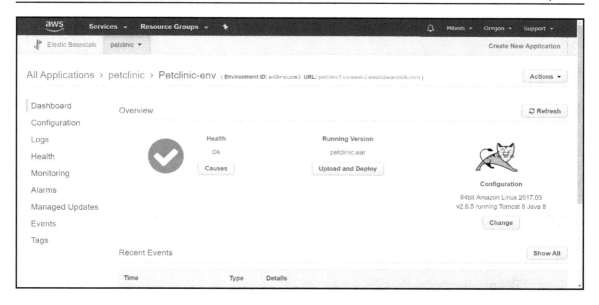

Now, we have an application that's ready to have traffic routed to it. Note the URL of the application.

Creating a CNAME resource record set

We can't create a CNAME resource record set for the root domain name. In our case, if the root domain is `cleanclouds.com`, then we can create `petclinic.cleanclouds.com` so that it routes traffic to the application that has been deployed in the Elastic Beanstalk environment. Let's set this up by going through the following steps:

1. Sign in to the AWS Management Console.
2. Go to the Amazon Route 53 console at `https://console.aws.amazon.com/ route53/` or select it from the **Services** menu.
3. Click on **Hosted zones**.
4. Select the hosted zone that has the domain name that we want to route traffic to for our Elastic Beanstalk environment.
5. Click on **Create Record Set**.

The following table describes all the parameters that are required to create a record set:

Parameter	Description
Name	Enter the domain name `petclinic.cleanclouds.net` for which you want to route traffic to your Elastic Beanstalk environment. The default value is the name of the hosted zone—that is, `cleanclouds.net`.
Type	CNAME, or canonical name.
Alias	No.
TTL (Seconds)	Default value of `300`.
Value	Type the domain name of the environment that you want to route traffic to.
Routing Policy	Accept the default value, **Simple**.

6. For **Name**, type the subdomain that will redirect to the PetClinic Elastic Beanstalk application.
7. Select a **CNAME** type.
8. In the **Value** field, provide the domain name of your Elastic Beanstalk environment, as shown in the following screenshot:

9. Click on **Create**.
10. Click on the newly created record set and verify the details.

The time that's required for changes to propagate to all Amazon Route 53 servers ranges from a couple of minutes to up to 30 minutes.

We can use name server values in the original domain provider for routing.

Summary

Well done! We are at the end of this chapter, so let's summarize what we have covered. First, we learned how to register a domain in the AWS Management Console. We also created an environment in AWS Elastic Beanstalk and then configured Route 53 for a web application.

In the next chapter, we will discuss AWS Direct Connect.

6
AWS Direct Connect

There are different ways to connect with AWS resources or to extend on-premises infrastructures in AWS and connect both networks. It is more about setting up a hybrid connection. One very important thing here is to connect to AWS resources that are effective for your usage. A few scenarios that directly come to mind are as follows:

- Hosting a web or app tier in AWS while a database is available on-premises
- Storing data or a database backup in S3

We can connect on-premises and AWS resources using a VPN connection over the public internet. What if we want to have a dedicated connection between AWS resources and an on-premises network and not the public internet? The answer is **Direct Connect**, which provides a dedicated connection to AWS resources using a Direct Connect partner, and here, no public internet is involved. In this chapter, we will cover AWS Direct Connect, which makes it easy to establish a dedicated connection between AWS and organization resources. The following topics will be discussed in this chapter:

- Introducing AWS Direct Connect
- An overview of AWS Direct Connect components

Introducing AWS Direct Connect

AWS Direct Connect provides a facility to create a dedicated network (private connectivity) connection between AWS and a traditional data center or on-premises network or colocation environment. The very first question should be: why it is required when we can access AWS resources over the internet? The answers follow:

- It is used to transfer data without using the public internet.
- It provides a secure and consistent network.
- A high-bandwidth network connection between the on-premises network and single or multiple VPCs is available in AWS. The next question is about capacity:
  - It provides 1 GBps and 10 GBps connections
- Compatibility with AWS services:
  - Amazon Elastic Compute Cloud
  - Amazon Virtual Private Cloud
  - Amazon Simple Storage Service

Now, here's another question: how does AWS Direct Connect works?

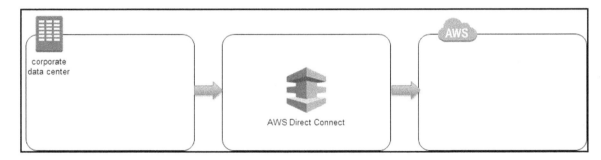

The following is the working for the preceding diagram:

- The on-premises router and the AWS Direct Connect router are connected with a cable.
- A virtual interface is created and connected to AWS services.
- The AWS Direct Connect location gives you access to AWS.

The following diagram shows the steps that you need to use to implement AWS Direct Connect:

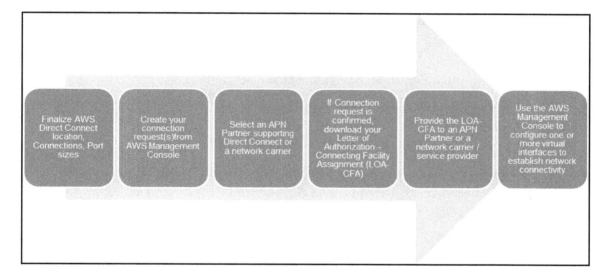

 All AWS services can be used with AWS Direct Connect.

In the next section, we will cover AWS Direct Connect components.

An overview of AWS Direct Connect components

Connection and virtual interfaces are the key components of AWS Direct Connect. We need to create a connection in an AWS Direct Connect location. Why do we need to create a connection? Because it is used to establish a network connection between on-premises and AWS.

 At the time of writing, AWS Direct Connect does not provide a **Service Level Agreement (SLA)**.

There are three ways to establish an AWS Direct Connect connection:

- By using an AWS Direct Connect location
- A member of the **AWS Partner Network** or a network carrier
- A hosted connection provided by a member of APN

 AWS Direct Connect is available in different geographic regions. For details, visit https://aws.amazon.com/directconnect/details/.

There are two options available in AWS Direct Connect for port speeds:

- **1 Gbps**: 1000BASE-LX (1310nm) over single-mode fiber
- **10 Gbps**: 10GBASE-LR (1310nm) over single-mode fiber

 APN partners support speeds of 50 Mbps, 100 Mbps, 200 Mbps, 300 Mbps, 400 Mbps, and 500 Mbps.

Let's look at how we can create a connection:

1. Go to `https://aws.amazon.com/` and log in. Keep some information at the ready, such as the port speed and the AWS Direct Connect location that you are going to connect to.

2. Click on **Services | Networking & Content Delivery | Direct Connect** or go to `https://console.aws.amazon.com/directconnect/`.

3. Select a region. This is the region where we want to connect to AWS Direct Connect:

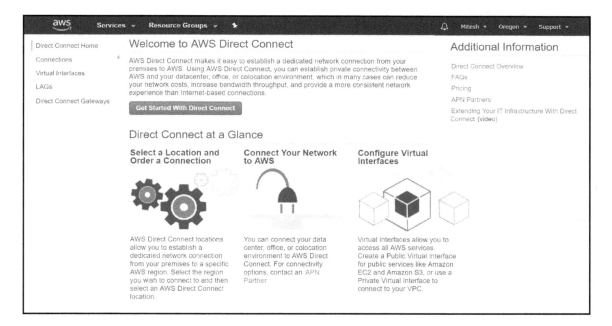

4. Click on **Get Started with Direct Connect**.

5. Provide the connection name.

6. Select **Location | Physical location**, where the cross-connection will be established. Select the **Port speed**. Click on **Create**:

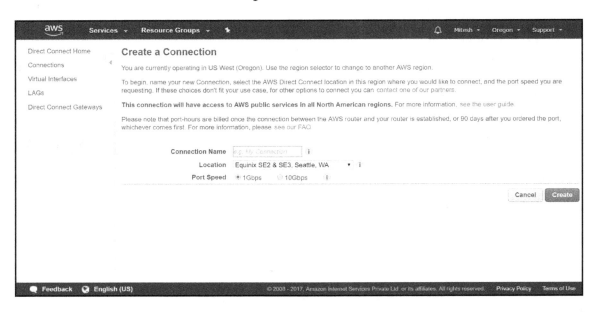

We can verify the newly created connection on the left sidebar. Select the connection and go to the summary section.

 We can use AWS Direct Connect if the network is not available at an AWS Direct Connect location using APN Partners. APN Partners help you extend a data center to an AWS Direct Connect location. For more details, go to https://aws.amazon.com/directconnect/partners/.

7. Select **I understand that Direct Connect port charges apply once**. Click **Accept this Connection** and click on **Accept Connection**. The next step is to configure two dedicated connections to AWS for failover, but this is optional.

 Each AWS Direct Connect connection includes a single dedicated connection between ports that are available on the on-premises router and an Amazon router on the other side.

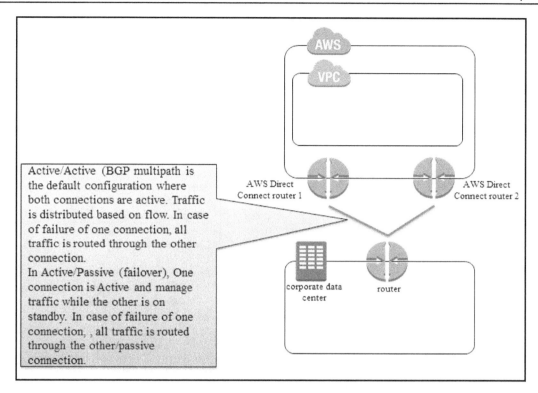

Once we are ready, after creating the AWS Direct Connect connection, the next step is to create virtual interfaces. There are two types of virtual interface:

Public virtual interface	Private virtual interface
It is used to connect to resources that are available in a virtual private cloud. We need one private virtual interface for each VPC so that we can connect to that VPC from the AWS Direct Connect connection. For a Public virtual interface, we need the following: • A unique **virtual local area network** (**VLAN**) tag • A public or private **Border Gateway Protocol** (**BGP**) **Autonomous System Number** (**ASN**) • A unique public IPv4 addresses (/ 30) • A virtual private gateway	It is used to connect to AWS services that are not in a virtual private cloud, such as Amazon S3.

• Go to `https://console.aws.amazon.com/directconnect/` or go to **Services	Networking & Content Delivery	Direct Connect	Virtual Interfaces**. • Select a **Connection** (existing physical connection). • Click on the **Actions** menu. • Select **Create Virtual Interface**. • Choose **Public Virtual Interface** for non-VPC services. • Provide a **Virtual Interface Name**. • Select **Virtual Interface Owner**; it can be your AWS Account or any other. • Provide a VLAN number. • For IPv4 BGP peer, select IPv4 (provide an IPv4 CIDR address). • For IPv6 BGP peer, select IPv6 (in this case, peer IPv6 addresses are automatically assigned from Amazon's pool of IPv6 addresses). • Provide a **Border Gateway Protocol (BGP) Autonomous System Number (ASN)** of gateway. • Select the auto-generate BGP key checkbox or provide your own BGP key. • Prefixes you want to advertise: provide the IPv4 CIDR destination addresses to which traffic should be routed over the virtual interface. • Click on **Continue** and then download your router configuration. • Go to `https://signin.aws.amazon.com` Click on **Virtual Interfaces** or go to **Services	Networking & Content Delivery	Direct Connect	Virtual Interfaces**. • Select the virtual interface that was created by you. • Click on the **Actions** menu and select **Download Router Configuration**. • It will open the **Download Router Configuration** dialog box. • Set the manufacturer of the router as **Vendor**, set the model of the router as **Platform**, and set the software version for the router as **Software**. • Click on **Download**. • Use the appropriate configuration for the router to connect to AWS Direct Connect; example router configuration files are available at `http://docs.aws.amazon.com/directconnect/latest/UserGuide/create-vif.html#vif-example-router-files`. • Once the virtual interface has been established, verify the AWS Direct Connect connection to the AWS Cloud and to Amazon VPC.	• Go to `https://console.aws.amazon.com/directconnect/` or go to **Services	Networking & Content Delivery	Direct Connect	Virtual Interfaces.** • Select a **Connection** (an existing physical connection). • Click on the **Actions** menu. • Select **Create Virtual Interface**. • Choose **Private Virtual Interface** for non-VPC services. • Provide a **Virtual Interface Name**. • Select **Virtual Interface Owner**; it can be your AWS account or any other. • Select **Virtual Private Gateway**. • Select a virtual private gateway to connect to. • Provide a VLAN number. • For IPv4 BGP peer, select IPv4 (provide a IPv4 CIDR address). • For IPv6 BGP peer, select IPv6 (in this case, peer IPv6 addresses are automatically assigned from Amazon's pool of IPv6 addresses). • Provide a **Border Gateway Protocol (BGP) Autonomous System Number (ASN)** of gateway. • Select the auto-generate BGP key checkbox or provide your own BGP key.

 For more details on virtual interfaces, visit `http://docs.aws.amazon.com/directconnect/latest/UserGuide/WorkingWithVirtualInterfaces.html`.

Another question might be: how can we connect to one or more VPCs and a customer network? The answer is through an AWS Direct Connect gateway. An AWS Direct Connect gateway can be used to connect one or more VPCs and customer networks using a private virtual interface over an AWS Direct Connect connection.

 Virtual private clouds can be in the same or different regions.

For the VPC, link the virtual private gateway with a Direct Connect gateway. Create a private virtual interface to connect AWS Direct Connect to the Direct Connect gateway. We can connect one or more private virtual interfaces to the Direct Connect gateway.

 For more details on Direct Connect Gateways, go to `http://docs.aws.amazon.com/directconnect/latest/UserGuide/direct-connect-gateways.html`.

Summary

Well done! We are at the end of this chapter, so let's summarize what we have covered. We understood the need for AWS Direct Connect, looked at an overview of Direct Connect, and then we covered how to start out with AWS Direct Connect using private and public virtual interfaces. In the next chapter, we will cover the shared responsibility model, identity and access management, security groups, and network ACL-related details. We will perform IAM best practices step by step and enable multifactor authentication to make AWS access more secure than before.

Security Best Practices

7

In this chapter, we will explore the ways in which we can secure resources in Amazon Web Services by using different options, such as IAM, security groups, and so on.

In AWS, security is not a responsibility of either AWS or the customer. Both are equally responsible for the security of resources based on the service model, such as IaaS and PaaS, that's used by the customer. Security is a shared responsibility in AWS.

AWS also provides authentication and authorization so that you can access AWS cloud resources in a controlled manner. AWS **Identity and Access Management** (**IAM**) allows you to configure secure access to AWS resources. It provides the facility to create users, groups, roles, and assign permissions to different such entities based on the policies that are available.

AWS also provides features such as security groups and network **Access Control Lists** (**ACLs**) to manage inbound and outbound traffic in a stateful and stateless manner at an instance and subnet level, respectively.

Network ACLs provide an additional layer of security other than security groups, and they both have allow and deny configuration available.

We will discuss the following topics in this chapter:

- The shared responsibility model
- Identity and Access Management
- Security groups
- Network ACLs

The shared responsibility model

Security can't be an afterthought. It is essential in the multi-tenant environment of the cloud.

It is clearly defined what the responsibility of AWS is as a service provider, and what the responsibility of a customer is as a consumer of AWS resources, and that helps to make the environment more secure. These responsibilities are provided in the following diagram:

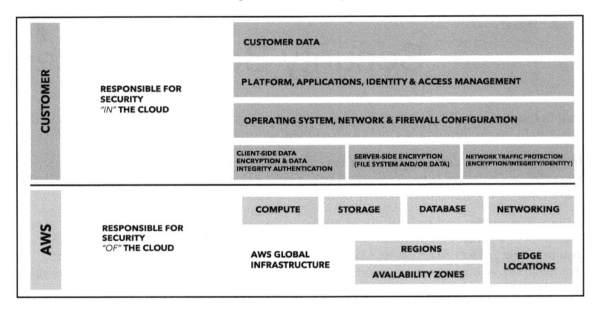

Reference: https://aws.amazon.com/compliance/shared-responsibility-model/

AWS is responsible for securing the cloud infrastructure, while the customer is responsible for configuring security in the cloud.

The responsibility of AWS and the customer may change based on the cloud service model that's used by the customer.

A **Platform as a Service (PaaS)** model demands more responsibility from AWS compared to **Infrastructure as a Service (IaaS)** because the customer has very little control over the overall environment in PaaS:

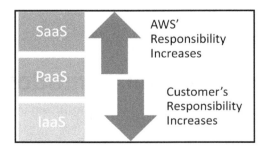

As you go down the service model, the customer's responsibility increases, and as you go up the service model, from IaaS to SaaS, AWS' responsibility increases.

Identity and Access Management

Identity and Access Management provides the facility to configure authentication and policy-based authorization. You can use AWS IAM services alongside the AWS Management Console, AWS command-line tools, AWS SDKs, and IAM HTTPS API.

With AWS IAM, it is easier to provide administration access and use resources with proper authentication and authorization. One of the most important features that's available is multi-factor authentication. When using multi-factor authentication, you need to provide a special code that's given by a configured virtual or physical device in addition to the required password. This feature makes access to your AWS account extremely secure.

One of the main reasons why AWS Identity and Access Management is popular is because of its ability to integrate with AWS services.

The following are the services that we have used in this book that work with IAM: Amazon VPC, Amazon CloudFront, AWS Direct Connect, Amazon Route 53, Amazon EC2, and AWS Elastic Beanstalk. To get more detailed information on AWS Services that work with IAM, go to `http://docs.aws.amazon.com/IAM/latest/UserGuide/reference_aws-services-that-work-with-iam.html`.

But is this the only reason why AWS Identity and Access Management is popular among customers?

No.

There is another reason too, and that is the pricing of AWS IAM. It is FREE.

Yes, you read that right. AWS IAM is free to use.

Why don't you want to use a service that provides authentication and authorization for FREE?

Recommendations are available on the AWS IAM dashboard itself. The following are some of the actions that can be done to make AWS resource access more secure:

- Don't use AWS account root user access keys—it is always better to avoid using an access key associated with an AWS account
- Create groups based on their requirements

- Create multiple users
- Assign policies to groups
- Assign users to specific groups
- Configure a strong password policy
- Provide an additional layer of security by providing AWS **Multi-factor Authentication** (**MFA**) for users

In this section, we'll create some groups, and then we will create users and assign each user to a specific group:

1. Go to **Services | Security, Identity & Compliance | IAM**.
2. Click on **Groups** and then click on **Create New Group**.
3. Specify a **Group Name** and click on **Next Step**:

In step 2, you need to attach a policy to the group:

1. Filter the relevant policies based on their requirements.
2. Click on **Next Step**:

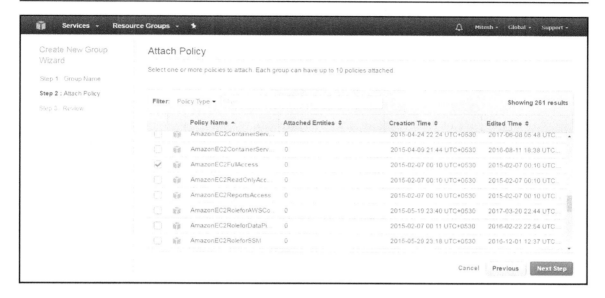

3. Review the **Group Name** and the policies associated with it.
4. Click on **Create Group**.
5. Similarly, create another group, called **Developers**.

Now, we have two groups available in the IAM dashboard:

It's time to create a user. Follow these steps to do so:

1. Go to **Services** | **Security, Identity & Compliance** | **IAM**, click on **Users**, click on **Create New User**, and provide a username.
2. If you want to add multiple users at a time, then click on **Add another user**. Select the access type that you want.
3. In the case of AWS Management Console access, provide a console password. You can also provide a rule to reset the password at the time of the user's first login.
4. Click on **Permissions**:

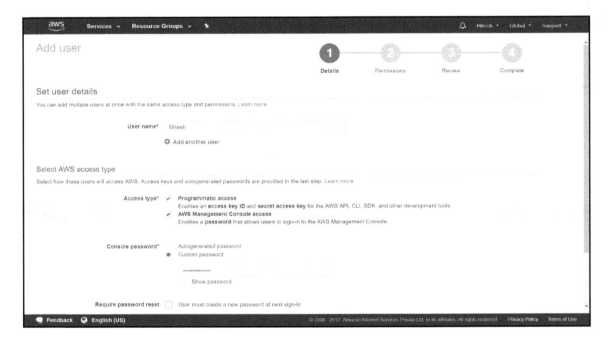

There are three ways to set permissions for the new user:

- Add users to a group so that all policies or permissions that are assigned to the group will be applicable to the user
- Copy permissions from the existing user
- Attach existing policies directly (however, it is better to avoid attaching policies directly to the user; it is better to create groups and assign policies to it)

In this case, we will assign the user to the group that we created earlier in this chapter, that is, Developers:

1. Click on **Review**.
2. Verify the **User details** that are available on the dashboard.
3. Click on **Create user**:

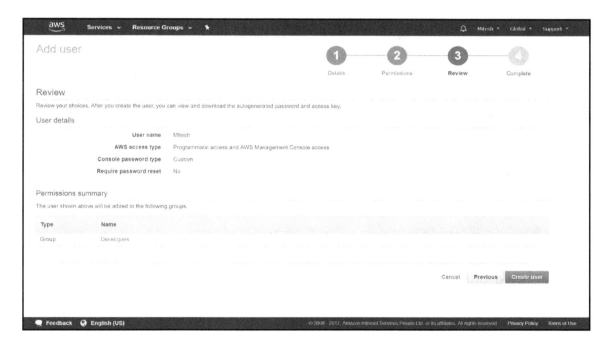

4. Click on **Close** once you get a **Success** message:

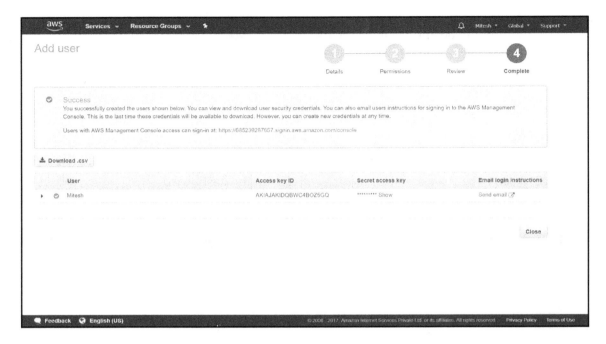

Now, let's go to the IAM dashboard and verify the security status that's provided. The users and groups are already in place, so the security status shows that **2 out of 5 is complet**e.

It is a best practice to delete access keys associated with the AWS Root account since they have all the necessary permissions to access resources and billing information.

It is advisable to use access keys that are available to an IAM User:

1. Click on **Delete your root access keys** and then click on **Manage Security Credentials**:

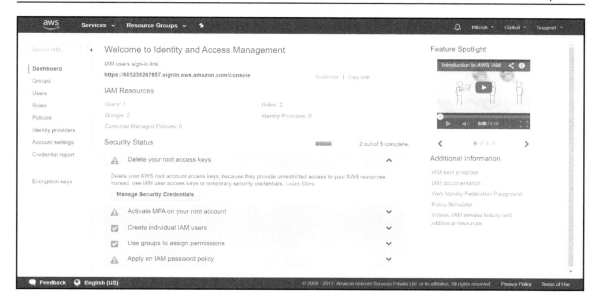

2. Click on **Continue to Security Credentials**:

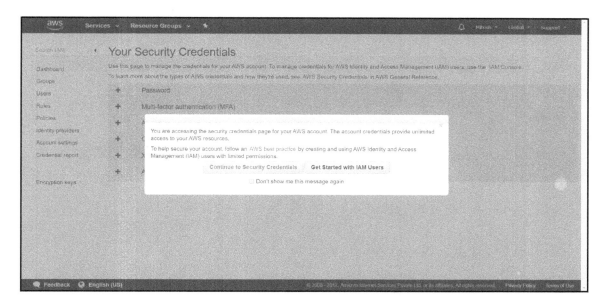

3. Delete all the access keys that are available in the list:

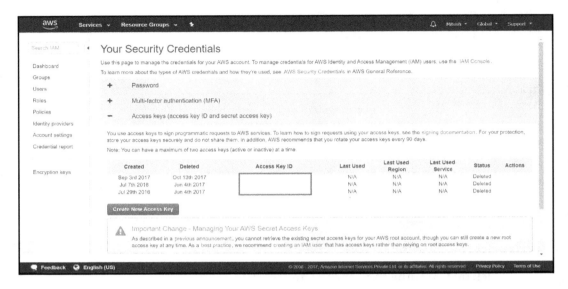

4. Go back to the IAM dashboard and check the security status. It should now show **3 out of 5 complete**:

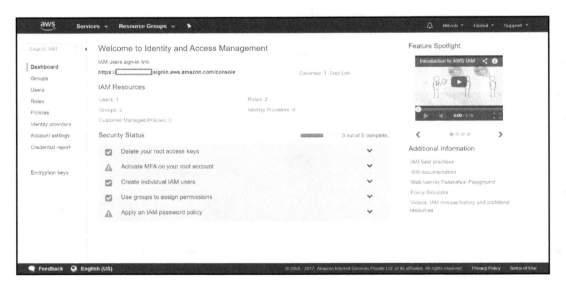

The password policy forces users to set strong passwords that are essential for the security of AWS resources.

Let's apply an IAM password policy:

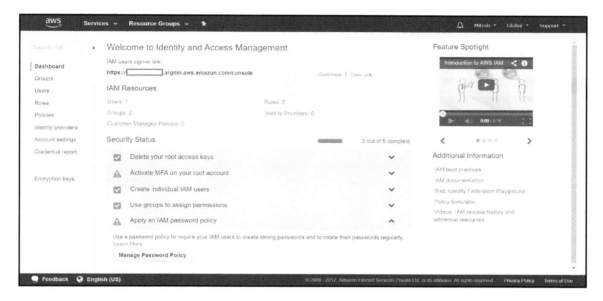

5. Select all the required options you need for a strong password policy and click on **Apply password policy**:

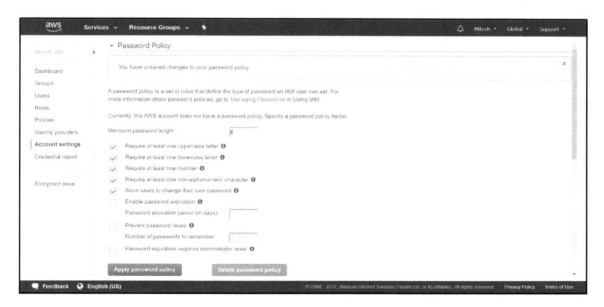

You will be provided with a message stating **Successfully updated password policy**.

6. Go back to the IAM dashboard and check its security status. It should now show **4 out of 5 complete**:

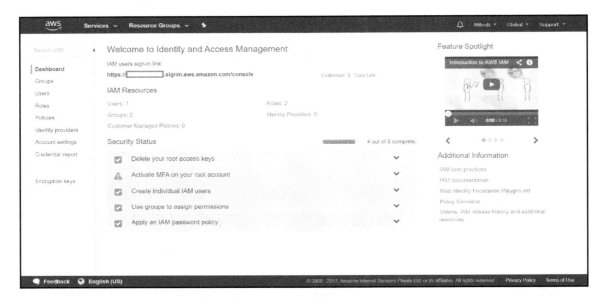

Now, it's time to activate MFA on your account:

7. Click on **Manage MFA**:

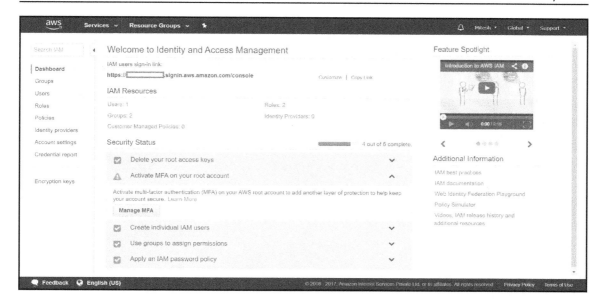

8. Select **A virtual MFA device** from the dialog box. Click on **Next Step**:

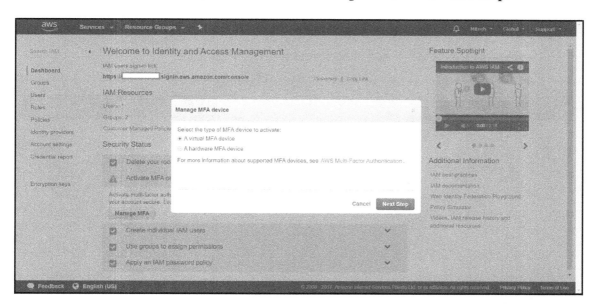

9. Click on **Next Step** again:

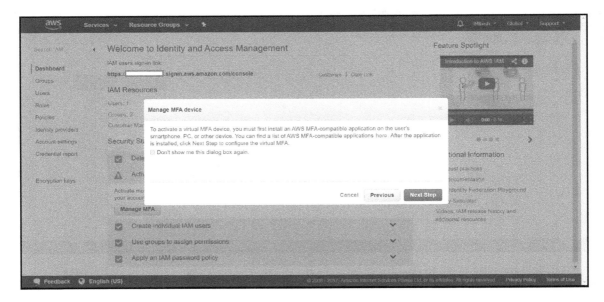

This will direct you to **MFA Form Factors**.

Observe all the devices and their features or capabilities:

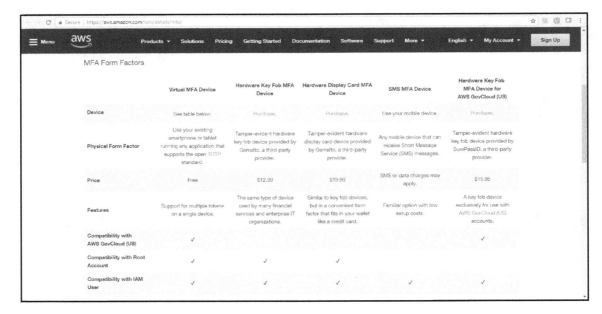

10. Scroll down the page and find **Virtual MFA Applications**:

The following is the QR code that we need to scan with our virtual MFA device:

Here, we will try out a virtual MFA device, that is, Google Authenticator:

1. In your Android smartphone, go to **Play Store**.
2. Find **Google Authenticator** in the Play Store and click on **Install**:

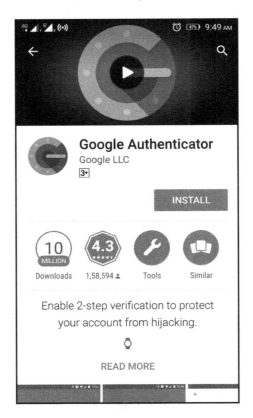

3. Once the application has been successfully installed on your mobile, click on **Open**.

4. Click on **Begin**:

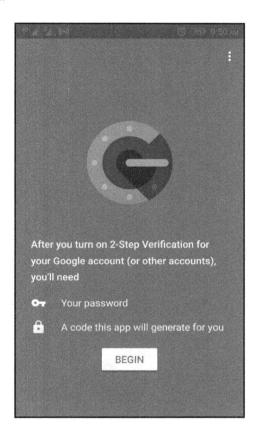

5. Swipe available screens:

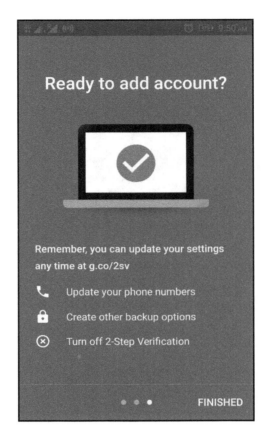

In Google Authenticator, the **Scan a barcode** option is available. We have a barcode available already:

1. Select scan a barcode.
2. Allow Google Authenticator to take pictures:

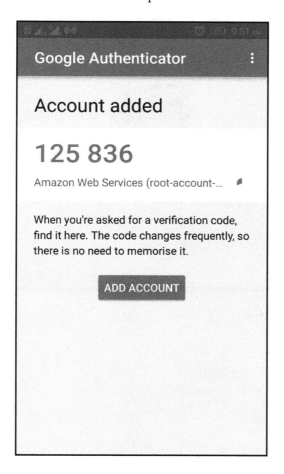

Once your account has been added, you will get the six-digit code that we need to provide in AWS. The six-digit code will change in Google Authenticator. Provide the two codes in AWS portal:

1. Click on **Activate virtual MFA**:

2. Once the MFA device has been successfully associated with the AWS account, click on **Finish**:

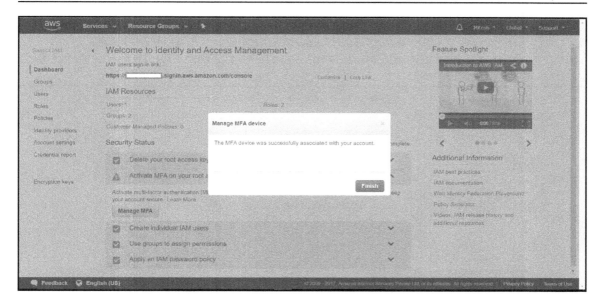

3. Go to the IAM dashboard in the AWS Portal and verify the security status. It should now say **5 out of 5 complete**:

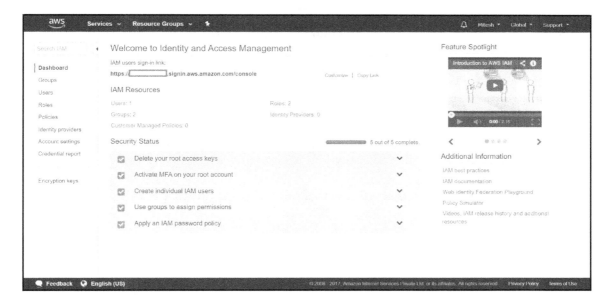

4. Now try to log in to the AWS account, once you provide the username and password, it will ask for additional authentication. Open your Google Authenticator app and provide the code here. Click on **Sign In**:

We have completed all the best practices that have been suggested by AWS for IAM.

A role is an important concept in AWS IAM. It can be assigned to anyone who needs access, and access keys are given dynamically. Another important feature is related to access using an AWS account. An IAM user in the same or different AWS account can use a role, as follows:

1. Click on **Roles** in **IAM Dashboard** and select **Create Role.**
2. Select the type of trusted entity you wish to use, which is AWS service in our case.
3. Choose the service that will use this role, which in our case is **EC2**. Click on **Next: Permissions**:

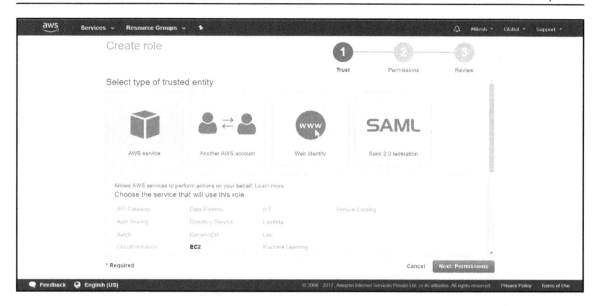

4. Attach permission policies.
5. Click on **Next: Review**:

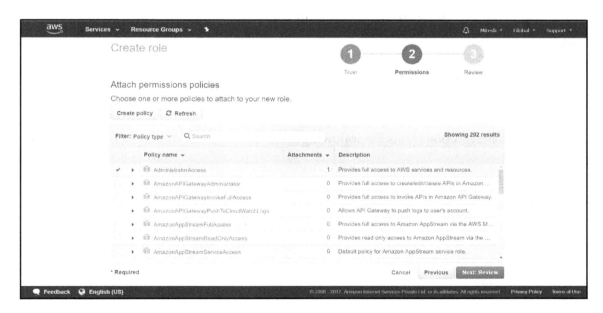

6. Provide **Role name** and **Role description.**
7. Click on **Create Role.**

Now, the role is ready to be assigned and used based on its requirements.

You can also create policies. Let's see how in the next section.

An overview of IAM policies

Policies are documents that help us define and assign permissions to a role, group, user, or AWS resource.

There are three types of policies in the AWS IAM service: AWS-managed, customer-managed, and inline policies.

An AWS-managed policy has the following features:

- It is easier to use for common access and assigning it to users, groups, and roles.
- It is a standalone policy that is created and administered by AWS.
- It has its own **Amazon Resource Names** (**ARNs**), which includes the policy name.
- It is useful for the following common use cases:
    - Administrator access
    - All Access except IAM
    - Service-level access, such as EC2 and S3
- Users can't change permissions that are defined in AWS-managed policies. Only AWS can update the permissions that are defined in an AWS-managed policy.
- The updated permissions are applied to all users, groups, and roles that the policy is attached to.

A customer-managed policy has the following features:

- Customer-managed policies are customized to suit the customer's environment
- It is a standalone policy that is created and administered by AWS Customer
- It has its own ARN, which includes the policy name
- Users can change permissions that are defined in customer-managed policies
- The updated permissions are applied to all users, groups, and roles that the policy is attached to

An inline policy has the following features:

- An inline policy is a policy that's embedded in a user, group, or role
- It is not a standalone policy but part of a user, group, or role
- You can create an inline policy and embed it within a user, group, or role

There are two ways to create the policy:

- By building a policy using **Visual editor**
- By creating a policy document using JSON editor

Go to **Services | Security**, and then **Identity & Compliance | IAM Dashboard**. Creating the policy consists of four main parts:

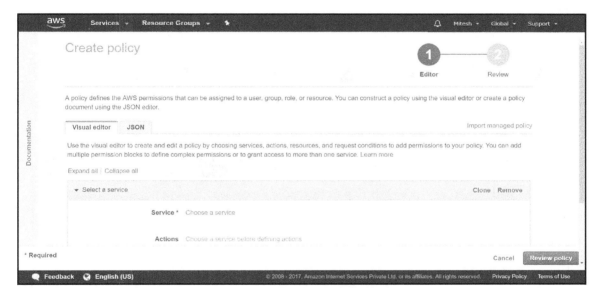

The first is **Service** (AWS service). Click on **Choose a service**:

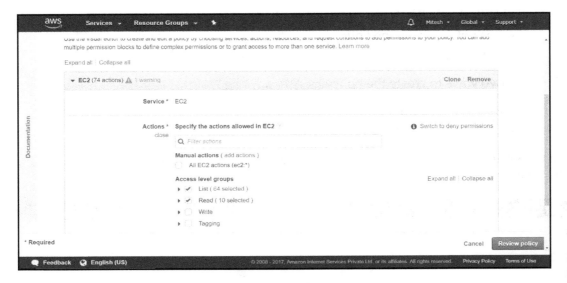

Then, there's **Actions** (choose a service before defining actions).

Select **EC2 actions**:

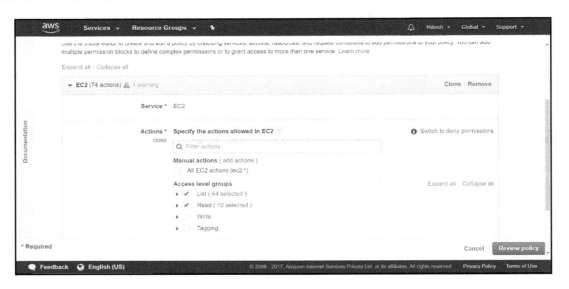

You can click on **Switch to deny permissions** to configure it as shown in the preceding screenshot.

Then, select the appropriate **Resources** (choose actions before applying resources).

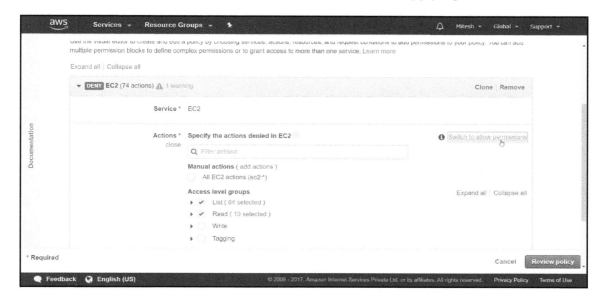

Finally, there's **Request Conditions** (choose actions before specifying conditions):

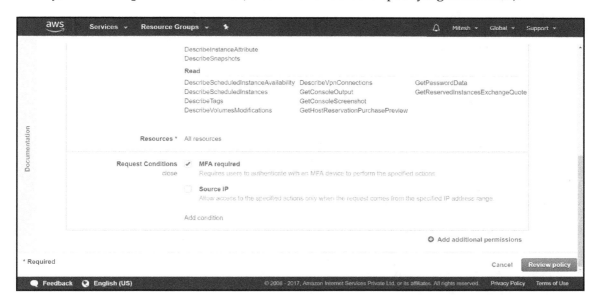

Click on the **JSON** editor to get the JSON script of the configured policy:

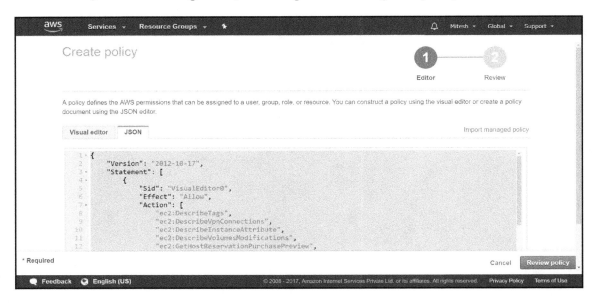

The following JSON script is displayed in the preceding screenshot:

```
{
"Version": "2012-10-17",
"Statement": [
{
"Sid": "VisualEditor0",
"Effect": "Allow",
"Action": [
"ec2:DescribeTags",
"ec2:DescribeVpnConnections",
"ec2:DescribeInstanceAttribute",
"ec2:DescribeVolumesModifications",
"ec2:GetHostReservationPurchasePreview",
"ec2:DescribeSnapshots",
"ec2:GetConsoleScreenshot",
"ec2:GetReservedInstancesExchangeQuote",
"ec2:GetConsoleOutput",
"ec2:GetPasswordData",
"ec2:DescribeScheduledInstances",
"ec2:DescribeScheduledInstanceAvailability",
"ec2:DescribeAccountAttributes"
],
"Resource": "*",
"Condition": {
```

```
"BoolIfExists": {
"aws:MultiFactorAuthPresent": "true"
}
}
}
]
```

Click on **Review policy**:

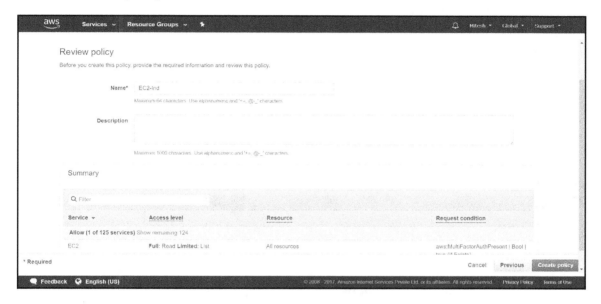

Click on **Create policy**.

Verify the newly created policy in the IAM dashboard and assign the role we created to utilize it:

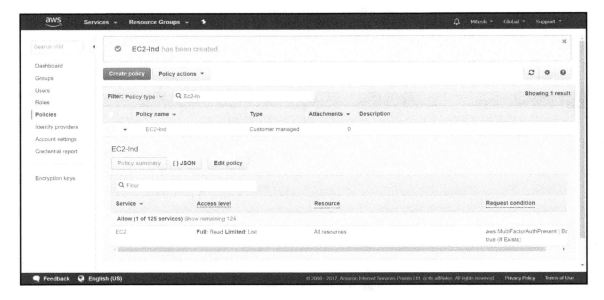

Let's create another policy that is related to S3.

Here's our scenario:

Create a policy that only allows actions such as creating a bucket and adding an object to the bucket:

- Creates a new bucket
- Adds an object to a bucket
- All read rights

Perform the following steps to complete the preceding actions:

1. Go to **Services | Security,** and then **Identity & Compliance | IAM Dashboard | Policies.**
2. Click on **Create policy.**
3. Select **S3** service from the list:

4. Click on **Actions**.

5. Select **List**, all the **Read** actions, and two **Write** actions:

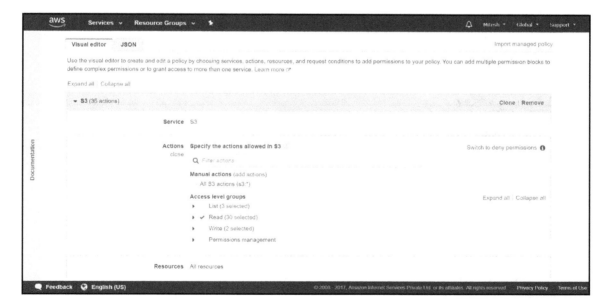

We have selected the following list actions:

- **ListAllMyBuckets**
- **ListBucket**
- **ListObjects**

6. Select all **Read** actions.
7. Select **CreateBucket** and **PutObject** for the **Write** actions.
8. Click on **Review policy**:

Provide a **Name** and **Description**.

9. Click on **Create policy**:

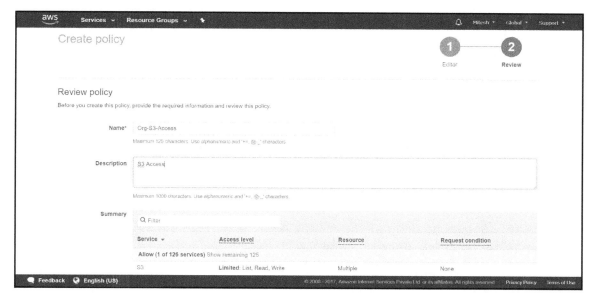

The policy will be created successfully.

Search for the policy, by name, in the list:

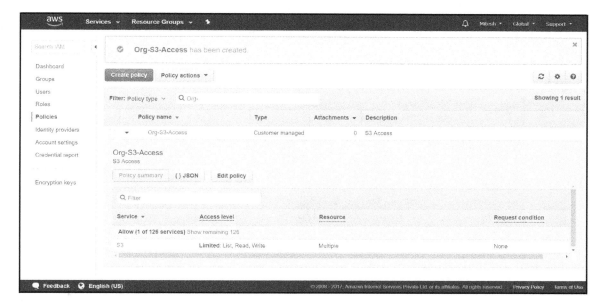

The following is the JSON block that was created for the policy we created:

```
{
  "Version": "2012-10-17",
"Statement": [
{
"Sid": "VisualEditor0",
"Effect": "Allow",
"Action": [
"s3:ListBucketByTags",
"s3:GetLifecycleConfiguration",
"s3:GetBucketTagging",
"s3:GetInventoryConfiguration",
"s3:GetObjectVersionTagging",
"s3:ListBucketVersions",
"s3:GetBucketLogging",
"s3:CreateBucket",
"s3:ListBucket",
"s3:GetAccelerateConfiguration",
"s3:GetBucketPolicy",
"s3:ListObjects",
"s3:GetObjectVersionTorrent",
"s3:GetObjectAcl",
"s3:GetBucketRequestPayment",
"s3:GetObjectVersionAcl",
"s3:GetObjectTagging",
"s3:GetMetricsConfiguration",
"s3:GetIpConfiguration",
"s3:ListBucketMultipartUploads",
"s3:GetBucketWebsite",
"s3:GetBucketVersioning",
"s3:GetBucketAcl",
"s3:GetBucketNotification",
"s3:GetReplicationConfiguration",
"s3:ListMultipartUploadParts",
"s3:PutObject",
"s3:GetObject",
"s3:GetObjectTorrent",
"s3:ListAllMyBuckets",
"s3:GetBucketCORS",
"s3:GetAnalyticsConfiguration",
"s3:GetObjectVersionForReplication",
"s3:GetBucketLocation",
"s3:GetObjectVersion"
],
"Resource": "*"
}
```

```
        ]
        }
```

Now that we have the policy available, let's create a user and assign a policy to it to verify its access.

1. Go to **Services** | **Security,** and then **Identity & Compliance** | **IAM Dashboard** | **Users.**
2. Click on **Add user.**
3. Provide a **User name** and **Access type.**
4. Click on **Next: Permissions**:

5. Click on **Attach existing policies directly.**
6. Find the recently created policy and select it.

7. Click on **Review**:

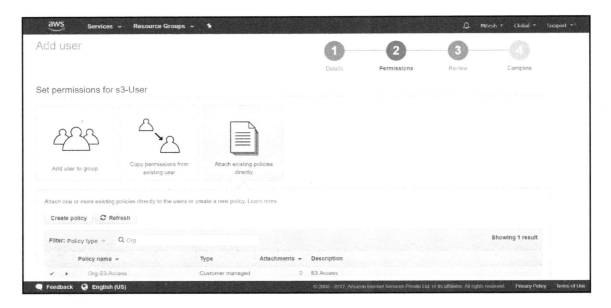

8. Click on **Create user**:

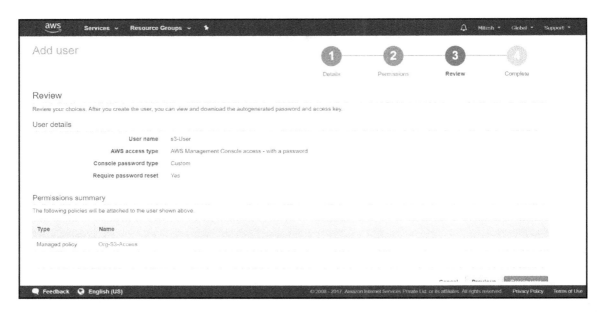

The user will have been created successfully:

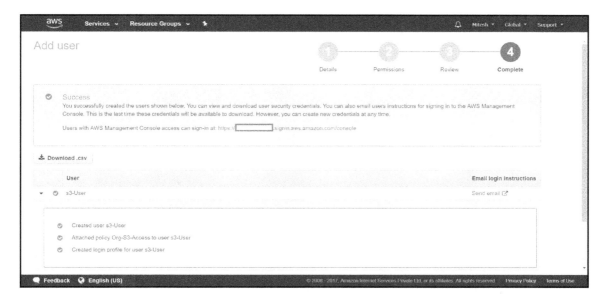

Go to the AWS Management Portal sign-in page and log in with the IAM URL that was provided in the IAM dashboard.

Provide the **IAM user name** and **Password** of the recently created user.

Click on **Sign In**:

Go to **Services** and click on **S3**.

Now, if you try and create a bucket, you will be allowed to do so.

However, if you try to delete a bucket, then it will throw an error since we haven't allowed delete permissions for any bucket while creating a policy:

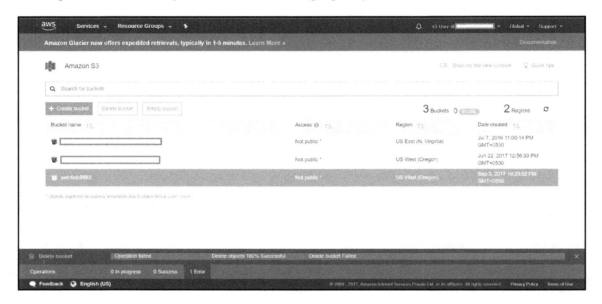

In the next section, we will discuss security groups.

Security groups

Security groups work like a firewall and manage inbound and outbound traffic based on configured rules at the instance level.

We can assign different security groups to different instances based on our needs. A default security group, that is, the default VPC security group that is available in both EC2 dashboard and VPC dashboard. Let's click on **Create Security Group**:

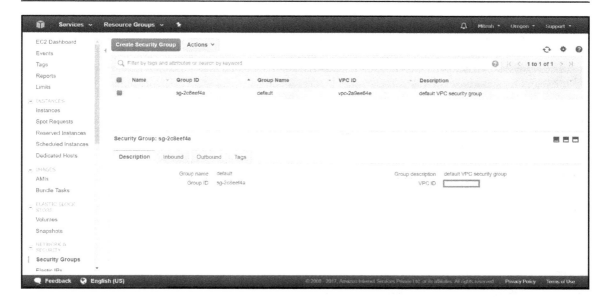

1. Provide a **Security group name** and select VPC. Then, click on **Create**:

2. Add an **Inbound** or **Outbound** rule based on your requirements and click on **Create:**

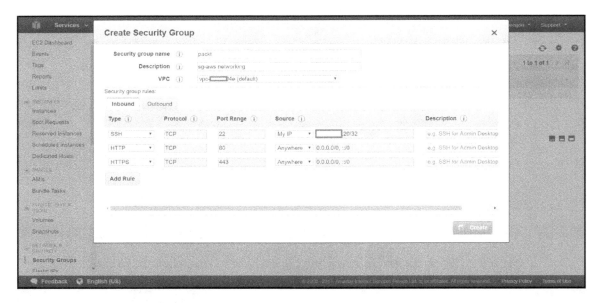

3. Verify the security group in the dashboard:

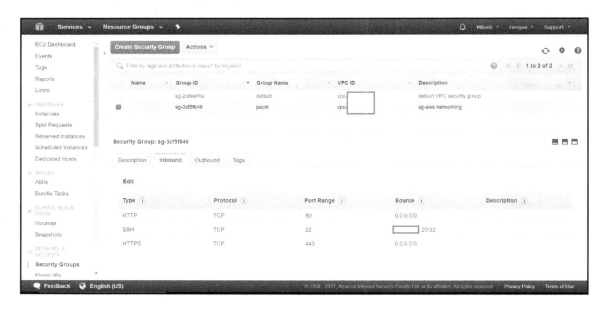

A security group is applicable at an instance level. Up to five security groups can be assigned to an instance. You can create 500 security groups per VPC (per region), 50 inbound or outbound rules per security group, and 5 security groups per network interface.

Network ACLs

Security groups work like firewalls and manage inbound and outbound traffic based on configured rules at the instance level. On the other hand, Network **Access Control Lists** (**ACLs**) provide an additional layer of security. Network ACLs work like firewalls and manage inbound and outbound traffic based on configured rules at the subnet level. Let's visit **Network ACLs** in the AWS Management Portal to find out more:

1. Go to the **VPC Dashboard** and verify the number of Network ACLs that are available:

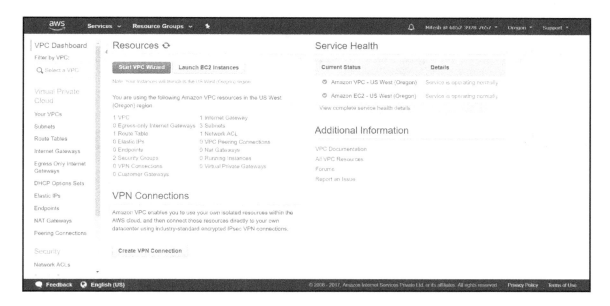

2. Click on **Network ACLs** in the left sidebar and check the **Summary** section. There are three subnets associated with it, as shown in the following screenshot:

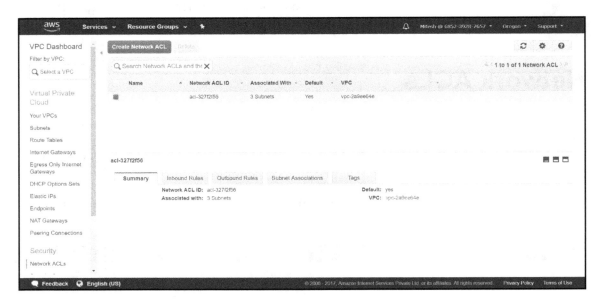

3. Go to the **Inbound Rules** tab and check whether there are any **Allow** or **Deny** rules available. Security groups only support allow rules:

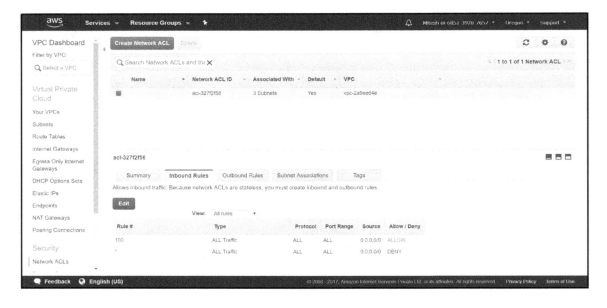

4. Go to the **Outbound Rules** tab and check whether there are
   any **Allow** or **Deny** rules available:

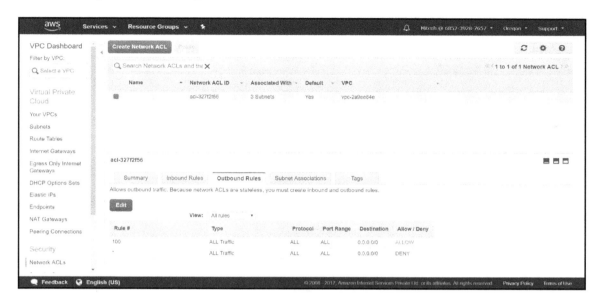

5. Go to the **Subnet Associations** tab, where there should be three subnets of the
   default VPC configured:

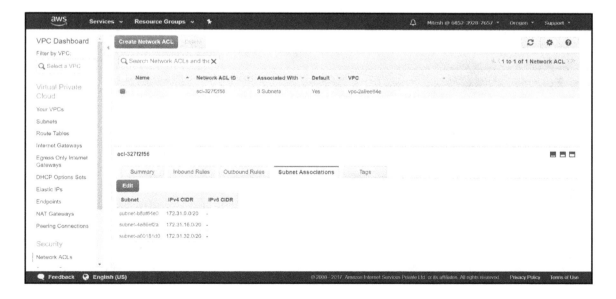

6. You can edit the number of subnets associated with the default VPC by clicking on the **Edit** button:

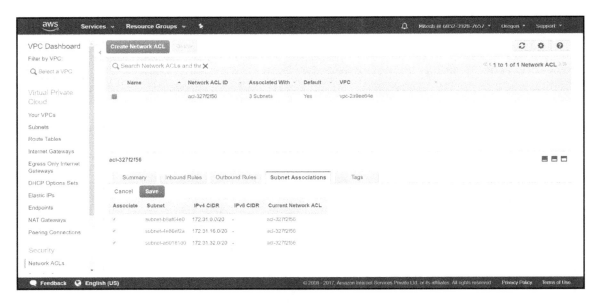

7. Now, click on **Create Network ACL**. Provide a name and select VPC. Click on **Yes, Create**:

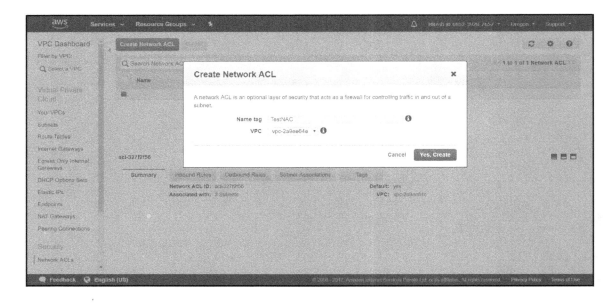

8. Verify the newly created Network ACL in a dashboard:

9. You can add inbound and outbound rules in a similar way to how you add them to security groups:

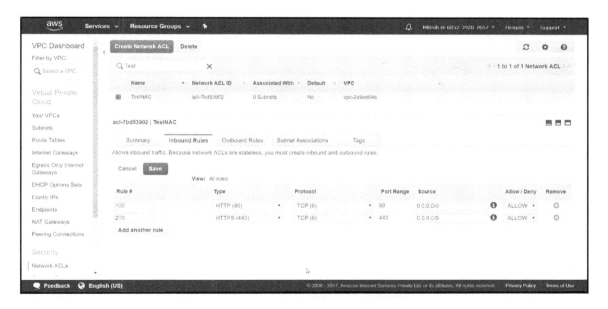

10. Save the changes that you've made in the inbound rules for the Network ACL:

11. Verify the rules that are available for the **Outbound Rules** tab and make any necessary changes based on your requirements or based on the policy of your organization:

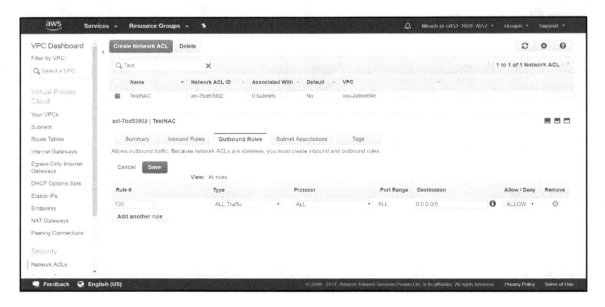

12. Click on the **Edit** button of the **Subnet Associations** tab:

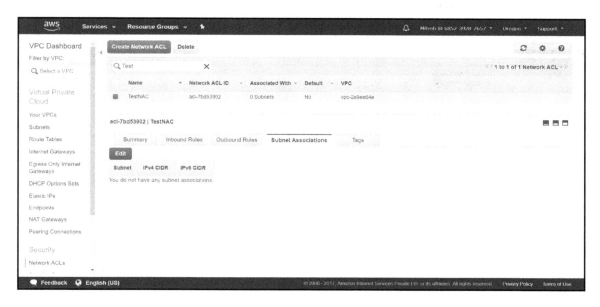

13. Select a specific subnet that you want to attach to the newly created Network ACLs and click on **Save**.

14. A subnet can't be associated with more than one Network ACL. As it is already associated with the default ACL, remove it first and then try to associate the subnet with the newly created Network ACL:

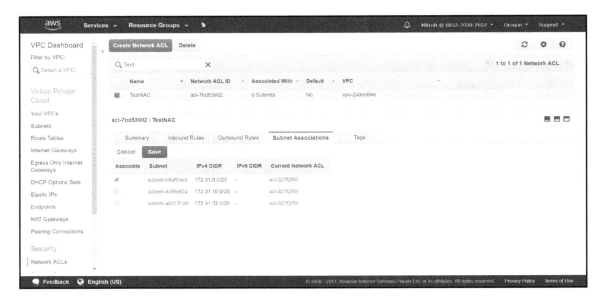

15. Verify **Subnet Associations**:

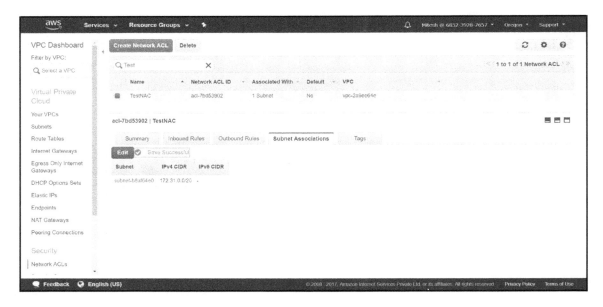

The Default Network ACL allows all inbound and outbound IPv4 traffic. Multiple subnets can be associated with a single Network ACL. Network ACLs are stateless, whereas security groups are stateful. To find out more about the Default Network ACL, visit `http://docs.aws.amazon.com/AmazonVPC/latest/UserGuide/VPC_ACLs.html#default-network-acl`.

Summary

Well done! We have to come the end of this chapter, so let's summarize what we have covered.

In this chapter, we understood the shared responsibility model between AWS and the customer to make the environment more secure. We also discussed Identity and Access Management in detail and implemented all the best practices that are available in the IAM Dashboard that were not compliant earlier. We configured multi-factor authentication for an AWS root account by using the Google Authentication application to make root account access more robust.

Finally, we discussed Security Groups and Network ACL, and also mentioned the differences between both of them.

In the next chapter, we will look at the day-to-day issues we encounter while creating and managing AWS resources.

8
Troubleshooting Tips

In this chapter, we will look at the day-to-day issues we encounter while creating and managing AWS resources, and then provide solutions for such issues.

Common problems and solutions

Let's try to describe the issues that we have faced when working with **Amazon Virtual Private Cloud (Amazon VPC)**:

- **Problem statement 1**: You have created an instance in a VPC, but you are unable to access the instance using SSH; you can't even ping the instance from your machine/laptop
- **Solution**: There are many reasons why you are unable to access the instance using SSH or unable to ping the AWS instance available in VPC

Let's discuss this:

1. If you are unable to access an instance that's been created in a VPC, then just for verification, check whether you are using the correct public DNS and IPv4 public IP:

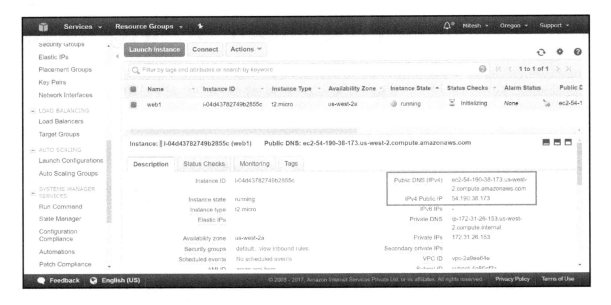

2. Put the correct public DNS and IPv4 public IP in PuTTY in the **Host Name (or IP address)** field to access the instance:

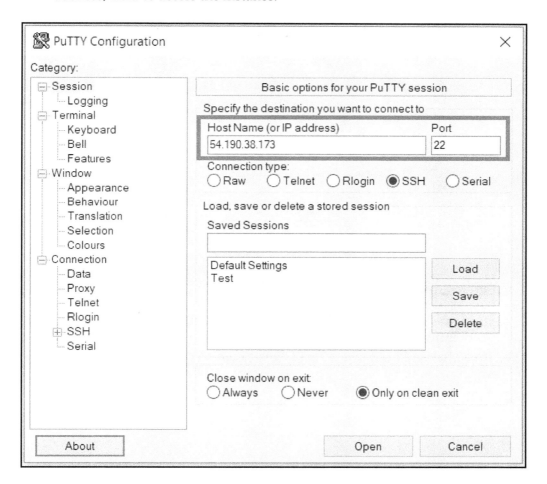

3. To access an instance that's available in a VPC, you need the key pair that you selected when creating the instance. You must have access to this access key:

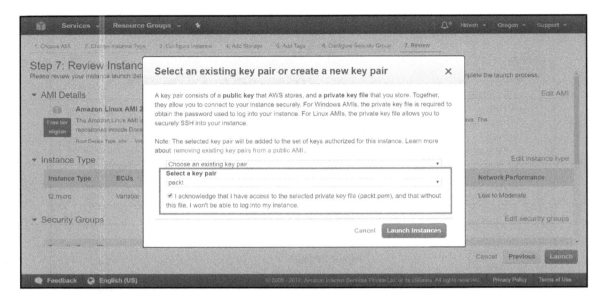

4. If you are using PuTTY, click on **Connection | SSH | Auth | Private key file for Authentication**.

5. If you have a PEM file, use PuTTYgen to convert it into a PPK file to access the instance using PuTTY:

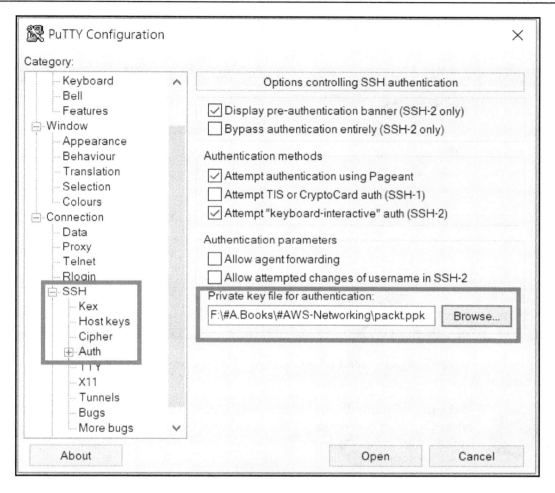

6. Check whether the security group associated with the instance has the inbound rule to accept the SSH Connection with the proper port from the correct source.
7. Go to the associated security group, click on **Inbound rule**, and add a rule.
8. Select **SSH** in type and provide 22 as the port number.

9. **Save** the security group, try to access the instance using PuTTY, and verify that the changes you made are working:

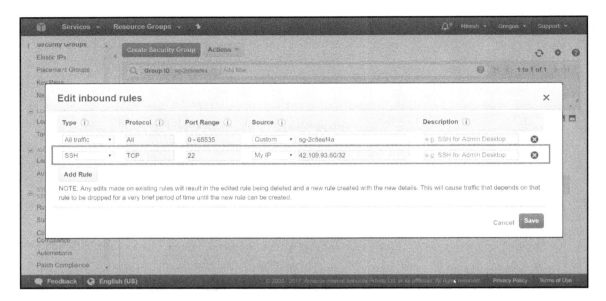

The preceding problems were faced when creating and accessing it for this book and are thus limited in nature.

 You can find more details in the article *How do I troubleshoot problems when connecting to an instance in a VPC?* which can be found at `https://aws.amazon.com/premiumsupport/knowledge-center/instance-vpc-troubleshoot/`.

Let's consider another scenario:

- **Problem Statement 2**: You have created an instance in Amazon VPC, but you are unable to ping the IP address or DNS from the command line
- **Solution**: The first thing you need to check is whether you can ping the instance using a public DNS

Let's solve this problem:

1. Go to **EC2 Dashboard**, select the instance, and note its public DNS and IPv4:

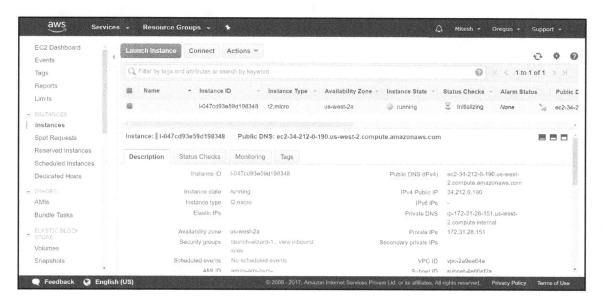

2. Try to ping the instance using a public DNS from the command line or Terminal:

```
Select Command Prompt                                          —  □  ×
Microsoft Windows [Version 10.0.15063]
(c) 2017 Microsoft Corporation. All rights reserved.

C:\Users\Mitesh>ping ec2-34-212-0-190.us-west-2.compute.amazonaws.com

Pinging ec2-34-212-0-190.us-west-2.compute.amazonaws.com [34.212.0.190] with 32 bytes of data:
Request timed out.
Request timed out.
Request timed out.
Request timed out.

Ping statistics for 34.212.0.190:
    Packets: Sent = 4, Received = 0, Lost = 4 (100% loss),
```

3. Click on the **Security Group** that was configured in the instance and click on **Edit inbound rules**.

4. Click **Add Rule** and **Save**. An ICMP rule needs to be added in the relevant security group:

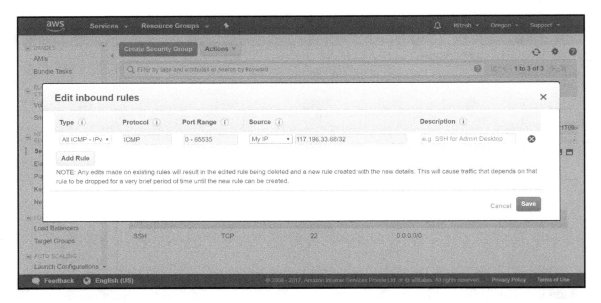

5. Verify that the modified security group with the **All ICMP** rule is enabled:

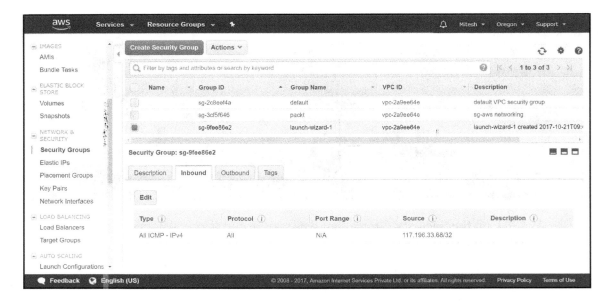

6. Try to ping the instance in the VPC using a public DNS or IP address:

```
C:\Users\Mitesh>ping ec2-34-212-0-190.us-west-2.compute.amazonaws.com

Pinging ec2-34-212-0-190.us-west-2.compute.amazonaws.com [34.212.0.190] with 32 bytes of data:
Request timed out.
Request timed out.
Request timed out.
Request timed out.

Ping statistics for 34.212.0.190:
    Packets: Sent = 4, Received = 0, Lost = 4 (100% loss),

C:\Users\Mitesh>ping ec2-34-212-0-190.us-west-2.compute.amazonaws.com

Pinging ec2-34-212-0-190.us-west-2.compute.amazonaws.com [34.212.0.190] with 32 bytes of data:
Reply from 34.212.0.190: bytes=32 time=362ms TTL=231
Reply from 34.212.0.190: bytes=32 time=376ms TTL=231
Reply from 34.212.0.190: bytes=32 time=390ms TTL=231
Reply from 34.212.0.190: bytes=32 time=407ms TTL=231

Ping statistics for 34.212.0.190:
    Packets: Sent = 4, Received = 4, Lost = 0 (0% loss),
Approximate round trip times in milli-seconds:
    Minimum = 362ms, Maximum = 407ms, Average = 383ms

C:\Users\Mitesh>ping 34.212.0.190

Pinging 34.212.0.190 with 32 bytes of data:
Reply from 34.212.0.190: bytes=32 time=313ms TTL=231
Reply from 34.212.0.190: bytes=32 time=313ms TTL=231
Reply from 34.212.0.190: bytes=32 time=313ms TTL=231
Reply from 34.212.0.190: bytes=32 time=430ms TTL=231

Ping statistics for 34.212.0.190:
    Packets: Sent = 4, Received = 4, Lost = 0 (0% loss),
Approximate round trip times in milli-seconds:
    Minimum = 313ms, Maximum = 430ms, Average = 342ms

C:\Users\Mitesh>
```

7. You can ping the instance after modification in the security group.

Check out the following scenario:

- **Problem Statement 3**: A VPC CIDR block overlaps with a pre-existing CIDR block in a subnet
- **Solution:** Open the VPC dashboard and perform the following steps

Let's get started:

1. Click on **Subnets** in the left sidebar.
2. Click on **Create Subnet**.
3. Provide a **Name tag** and select custom **VPC**.
4. Provide an IPv4 CIDR block based on the VPC CIDRs that have been configured for a custom VPC.

Let's create a subnet with a /28 subnet mask. Remember that we already have a VPC with a 10.0.0.0/24 CIDR.

Click on **Yes, Create**:

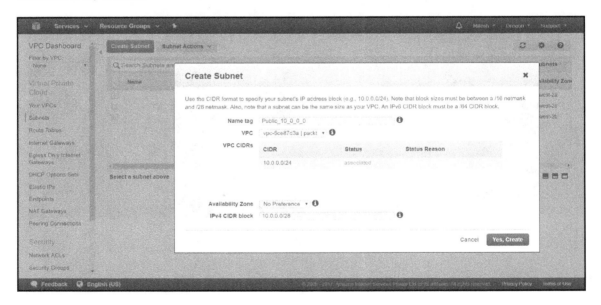

Now, you have a subnet with a `10.0.0.0/28` CIDR block.

In **VPC Dashboard**, when you click on **Subnets** in the left sidebar and try to **Create Subnet**, you may face an issue regarding the **Classless Inter-Domain Routing (CIDR)** subnet.

While creating a subnet, provide a **Name tag** and select a custom VPC. You need to make an IPv4 CIDR block available based on the VPC CIDRs that have been configured for the custom VPC.

Let's create a subnet with the `/28` subnet mask:

1. Provide a CIDR block that doesn't overlap with pre-existing CIDR blocks for the subnet you are trying to create:

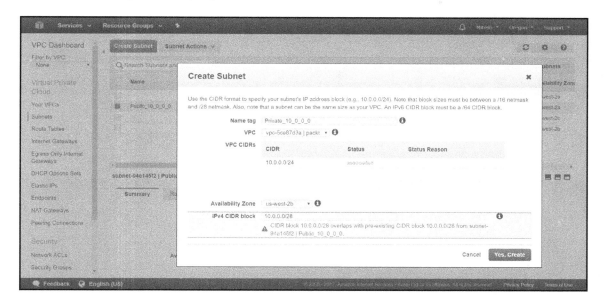

2. Try creating another one:

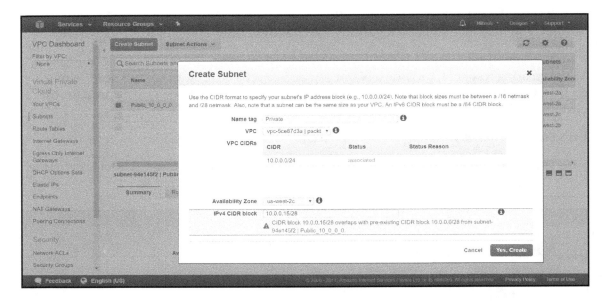

It doesn't work. The reason is that `/28` provides 16 addresses. We
used `10.0.0.0/28` for a public subnet that utilizes 16 addresses, `10.0.0.0/28`
to `10.0.0.15/28`:

3. Go to the **Subnets** section and verify that the newly created subnet is associated with the custom VPC.

To understand CIDR blocks, IP ranges, subnet masks, and the number of IP addresses better, refer to the following table:

CIDR Block	IP Range	Subnet Mask	IP Quantity
10.0.0.0/32	10.0.0.0 - 10.0.0.0	255.255.255.255	1
10.0.0.0/31	10.0.0.0 - 10.0.0.1	255.255.255.254	2
10.0.0.0/30	10.0.0.0 - 10.0.0.3	255.255.255.252	4
10.0.0.0/29	10.0.0.0 - 10.0.0.7	255.255.255.248	8
10.0.0.0/28	10.0.0.0 - 10.0.0.15	255.255.255.240	16
10.0.0.0/27	10.0.0.0 - 10.0.0.31	255.255.255.224	32
10.0.0.0/26	10.0.0.0 - 10.0.0.63	255.255.255.192	64
10.0.0.0/25	10.0.0.0 - 10.0.0.127	255.255.255.128	128
10.0.0.0/24	10.0.0.0 - 10.0.0.255	255.255.255.0	256

If we try `10.0.0.16/28`, it works. Click on **Yes, Create**.

 Valid CIDR block sizes must be between a `/16` and `/28` netmask.

Consider the following scenario:

- **Problem Statement 4**: An AWS account was suspended.
- **Solution**: An AWS account is suspended if timely payment isn't made, even after multiple mail notifications from AWS. AWS suspends the account for non-payment, and it also sends a notice in the form of a mail notification to the effect that the account is suspended.

How do we reactivate it? Open a support case in the AWS Support Center. Then, log into your AWS Management Console and go to `https://console.aws.amazon.com/billing/home#/paymenthistory`:

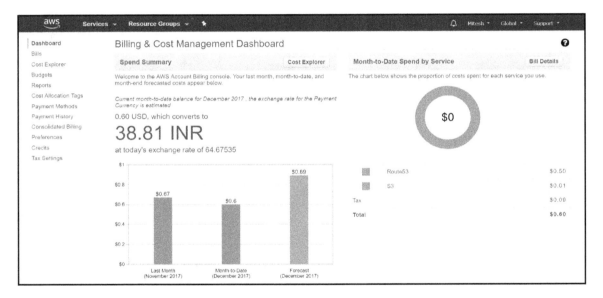

Click on **Pay Now** for all outstanding charges. Payment will be made via the default payment method that you've configured:

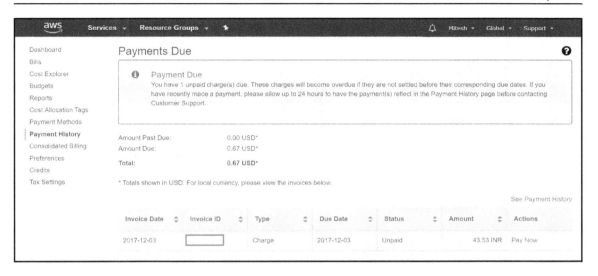

Reply to the support case once all bills are paid, and the account will be reactivated.

Check out the following scenarios:

- **Problem Statement 5**: You are not subscribed to the AWS service. Please see `http://aws.amazon.com`.
- **Solution**: The likely reason is that your account has expired. Go to `http://aws.amazon.com` and open a new account.
- **Problem Statement 6**: `AutoScalingGroup` not found.
- **Solution**: It is possible that you deleted the Auto Scaling group. Create a new Auto Scaling group to fix this problem.
- **Problem Statement 7**: The key pair does not exist. Launching an EC2 instance failed in ELB.
- **Solution**: It is possible that you deleted the key pair that can be used while launching the EC2 instance. Get the list of available commands from the AWS Management Console. Create a new key pair. Create a new launch configuration and update your Auto Scaling group with the new launch configuration.
- **Problem Statement 8**: How do we recover access keys?
- **Solution**: Each access key has two parts. The first is the access key identifier, which you can get in the IAM console. The second part is the secret access key, which is only available when we initially create the access key. There is no way to retrieve it later. If it is lost, you can recreate another key and use that.

To find access keys, go to **Services** | **Security, Identity & Compliance** | **IAM** | **Dashboard** | **Security Status** | **Delete your root access keys** | **Manage Security Credentials** | **Continue to Security Credentials** | **Access keys (access key ID and secret access key)**:

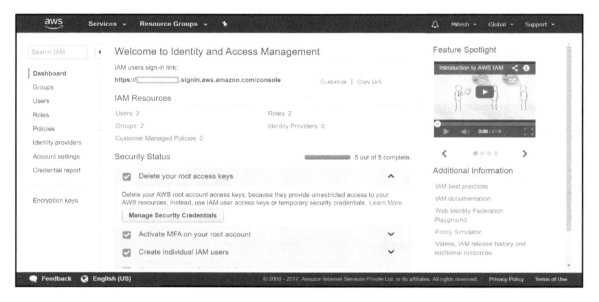

You can also click on **Username** in the top bar and then select | **My Security Credentials** | **Access keys (access key ID and secret access key)**.

Verify that the access keys are available in the portal:

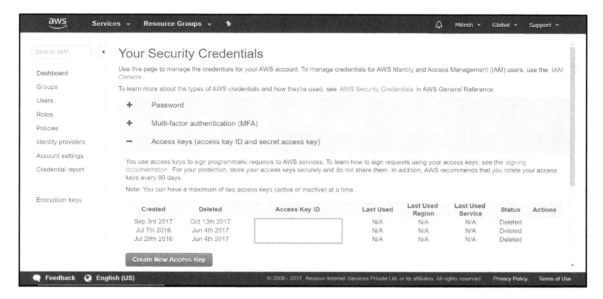

In the next section, we will look at a problem related to unhealthy targets for Elastic Load Balancing.

Unhealthy targets for Elastic Load Balancing

While using Elastic Load Balancing, you may face issues when accessing an application.

Problem Statement: The targets in the **Target Groups** that are assigned to Elastic Load Balancing are unhealthy.

The solution to the preceding problem statement is as follows:

1. Check whether all the targets serving the Elastic Load Balancing are healthy. Use port 80 to verify the listener:

2. Go to the **Target Groups** assigned to Elastic Load Balancing.
3. In the **Targets** tab, verify the registered targets and make sure that the targets have the port that has Tomcat running on it. In this case, Tomcat is running on 8080:

4. Go to **Health checks** and edit the path where the application is accessible.
5. Configure **Timeout**, **Interval**, and **Success codes**:

6. Wait until the interval time and check the status of **Targets** again.

Unable to connect to Tomcat server

If you are using Tomcat as a web server for application deployment, you must be able to access Tomcat from the instance that was created in the VPC:

- **Problem Statement**: You created an instance, installed the Tomcat web server, and copied the WAR file into the `webapps` directory of the Tomcat installation. By default, Tomcat works on port `8080`. Try to access Tomcat using the public DNS and the `8080` port. You can't access it:

The solution to the preceding problem statement is as follows:

1. **Edit inbound rules** in the security groups associated with the instance that was created in the VPC and then add a rule for port `8080` from the specific source, or from anywhere, based on your requirements:

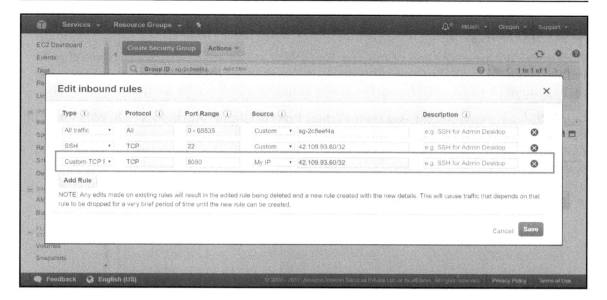

2. Try to access Tomcat using the public DNS and port `8080`:

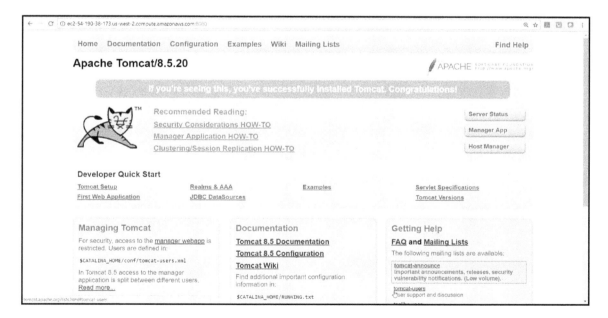

Now, you will be able to access Tomcat if it is running.

Summary

Well done! We are at the end of this chapter, so let's summarize what we've covered so far. In this chapter, we tried to give solutions to issues that can occur during day-to-day management of some AWS resources. It is a limited list and not exhaustive.

In this book, we covered the **Amazon Virtual Private Cloud** (**Amazon VPC**). We looked at how to create VPCs using a wizard and without. We also covered how to deploy AWS Elastic Beanstalk instances in the custom VPC we created. This book also discusses auto-scaling and Elastic Load Balancing. Security best practices were covered in detail, and include IAM best practices; we also configured multi-factor authentication for an AWS account. We briefly covered the AWS Route 53 and Direct Connect topics as well.

Other Books You May Enjoy

If you enjoyed this book, you may be interested in these other books by Packt:

AWS Networking Cookbook
Satyajit Das, Jhalak Modi

ISBN: 978-1-78712-324-3

- Create basic network in AWS
- Create production grade network in AWS
- Create global scale network in AWS
- Security and Compliance with AWS Network
- Troubleshooting, best practices and limitations of AWS network
- Pricing model of AWS network components
- Route 53 and Cloudfront concepts and routing policies
- VPC Automation using Ansible and CloudFormation

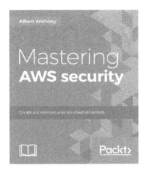

Mastering AWS Security
Albert Anthony

ISBN: 978-1-78829-372-3

- Learn about AWS Identity Management and Access control
- Gain knowledge to create and secure your private network in AWS
- Understand and secure your infrastructure in AWS
- Understand monitoring, logging and auditing in AWS
- Ensure Data Security in AWS
- Learn to secure your applications in AWS
- Explore AWS Security best practices

Leave a review - let other readers know what you think

Please share your thoughts on this book with others by leaving a review on the site that you bought it from. If you purchased the book from Amazon, please leave us an honest review on this book's Amazon page. This is vital so that other potential readers can see and use your unbiased opinion to make purchasing decisions, we can understand what our customers think about our products, and our authors can see your feedback on the title that they have worked with Packt to create. It will only take a few minutes of your time, but is valuable to other potential customers, our authors, and Packt. Thank you!

Index